Praise for *Still Rising*:

"Read this book. Simply and urgently, read this book. PHDs and theologians with decades of lectures cannot better the truths revealed in the endless suffering this family endured. Truths, if absorbed, will open the reader's comprehension of the true Christ. This writing reduces to ashes the flippant philosophies of the health-and-wealth, self-serving doctrines that crumble under the weight of reality. We learn through the things we suffer. If you don't believe it... ask Jesus. He learned obedience through the things He suffered."

- **Dave Roever**, President & Founder, Roever Foundation, Fort Worth, TX

"This is a story written from the lives of a couple who have walked through the greatest battle any parent could ever face. It's a story that reveals their greatest hopes and dreams, but also, their heartbreaking loss. Richard and Daphne Gaspard bravely share from their lives and the life of their daughter Katie, teaching us how to hold on to God when everything in life is spinning completely out of control.

Their story is real and powerfully authentic. It has taught me more than they will ever know... from their relentless hope which shines bright in the depth of adversity, their song that rises beautifully and refuses to be silenced, their faith that has grown stronger to face every battle, and the magnificent love they share that has only grown deeper.

This book will encourage every reader - those who are currently going through the hardest places in life and for those who are walking with them, as well as everyone who may go through hard places. Katie's life continues to instruct us to love and trust God, and to live for Him with complete abandon, with every single breath that we are given while here on Earth. Truly, her life and legacy are *Still Rising*."

- **Helen Burns**, Pastor, Relate Church, Surrey, BC, Canada

"I have always loved Richard and Daphne. This book will make you love them, too, I'm sure. But more importantly, I hope it helps you see how much Jesus loves you and the joy you can find in loving Him through any circumstance. The Gaspard family experienced pain that is beyond my comprehension. And yet, what I see in their story is something even more inexplicable - the overwhelming beauty that comes from trusting God regardless of what life brings."

- **DeLynn Rizzo**, Association of Related Churches, Birmingham, AL

"With *Still Rising*, my friends Richard and Daphne Gaspard have given a voice to both grief and hope at the same time. This is not simply a chronicle of life and death, it is a reminder of what faith and trust in God really looks like.

Still Rising simultaneously extends hope to those in a moment of great hardship and counsel to those wanting to respond with compassion. It is a must-read for anyone desiring to be found among those the scripture characterizes as *the just* (who) *live by faith.*"

- **Jeff Ables**, Lead Pastor, Crossroads Church, Lafayette, LA

"How can a tale both rip into our heart of hearts while also digging us deeper into God's love? Richard and Daphne endured a parent's worst nightmare, yet by clinging to their only anchor in the storm, they impart a hero's faith.

Even renowned theologian C.S. Lewis asked, 'If God is good and all-powerful, why does he allow his creatures to suffer pain?' Richard and Daphne grapple with this question through the excruciating journey of their daughter's illness. Their story is a must-read for all who yearn for deeper understanding of faith even when God doesn't "fix things" like we think He should.

Gut-wrenchingly honest and insightful, Richard and Daphne Gaspard's story is for all of us who grapple with unanswered questions and aching emotional wounds."

- **Chana Keefer**, #1 best-selling author of *Servant of the King: Memoir of Modern Apostle Kemper Crabb*, Agua Dulce, CA

"Life can be tough, and no matter who we are, we don't have all the answers. Although I watched the Gaspards' story unfold in real life, I can't say I truly had a grasp of their struggles, needs, or longings until I read this book. As a result of it, I not only see what I could have done differently, but I am better prepared to help others today than ever before.

What started as a story turned into a manual for me, and I believe every pastor needs to read this story. It is honest, raw, and such a reminder that God hasn't called us to have all the answers as much as to be there for those on this journey called life."

- **David Baudoin**, President, Life Counseling, Lafayette, LA

*A Story of Strength, Weakness,
and Unexpected Healing*

RICHARD & DAPHNE GASPARD

To our sweet Katie Mac, the bravest and strongest girl we've ever met. We miss you terribly, but we're so very thankful that God chose us to be your parents.

One day we will meet again, but until then, we are *Still Rising*.

ACKNOWLEGMENTS

We never intended to write a book on suffering. We never intended to write a book about losing our daughter. We never intended to write a book chronicling difficult seasons.

Heck, we never intended to write a book at all.

We never dreamed we'd find ourselves in a place where we'd be experts on any of it. But we also never dreamed we'd have such amazing support from such amazing people.

To Kylie, we love you more than life itself. Thank you for putting your needs on the back burner for your sister's sake. Thank you for being selfless during what should've been your time to get all the attention. We never heard you complain - not once. You were a bright light in Katie's life, especially during her last years. We always told you that she was your biggest fan, but honestly, we were, and still are. We are still so very proud to be your parents.

To Marvin and Debbie, we know it must have been difficult to watch us from afar, and we know your ministry assignment made it difficult to get away, but we are so appreciative of the two of you. We are grateful for the time you were able to spend with us, all the help and support you offered, the phone calls, and nursing advice. Katie always looked forward to visits from her beloved Nana and Popee, and her last two years in Houston were no exception.

To Ray and Lou, as part of the great cloud of witnesses, cheering us on, you certainly had a front-row seat of what our journey looked like, but from an eternal perspective. Thank you for walking out your faith in front of the Gaspard children long before Kylie and Katie were born. To Lou, especially, thank you for setting the bar with regards to caring for a patient with a long-term sickness. Take care of our little girl, your granddaughter, in Heaven.

To Kraig ("Pops") and Laura, thank you for being our girl's second home. She loved you, and we often wondered if she'd rather just as soon live at your house. Thank you for your friendship. Avery, words cannot express the gratitude we feel for you. Katie loved you beyond belief. She always thought of you as her best friend, and over the last few years, you really proved that you were.

To Bryan and Jeri, we don't know how we could have made it without the two of you. To sum up your selflessness and friendship in a couple of sentences within a book's acknowledgments seems to be trite, in comparison. Bryan, thank you for empowering your beautiful wife to be who she is: a servant. Jeri, you are the true picture of love, friendship, and compassion. You are the true picture of Jesus' heart for people in need.

To Vance and Kari, no amount of thanks is ever enough. You were on our team from Day One. Thanks for loving our girls and encouraging them to be fierce arrows in faith. No girl ever has had an adopted aunt and uncle as great as the two of you.

Tammy, Sonia, Beau and Kindra, Jason and Candace, Derek, Daniel, Perry, Steve, and Coy, your encouragement meant everything to us. The phone calls, texts, Facebook messages, deep conversations (venting sessions), and support will never be forgotten.

To all of our Lafayette friends who were with us on this journey, whether or not we've mentioned you in this book, you know who you are, and thank you. Also, to Crossroads Church, First Baptist Church, The Family Church, and all the other wonderful Acadiana-based ministries, the support we felt from you kept us going through the worst of times. We knew we had an army praying for us, and we knew we were being carried on those prayers. Thank you a million times over.

To Ryan and Amy, Darren and Sera, Lashund, Tad and Karen, Yvonne, Brenda, Sharon, David and Mary, James and Katherine, Guy, and the rest of our Texas family, thank you for adopting us, caring for us, spending time with us, and showing the love of Christ in a real and tangible way. Cajuns love to brag on their hospitable spirit, but you did it, Texas-style.

To John and Helen, thank you for pastoring us when you didn't even realize it. You provided so much wisdom and love before, during, and after Katie's battle. We love you.

To Jeff and Donna, thank you for preparing us for the trial of our lifetime. You have made an indelible mark on our lives. Sitting under your teachings on faith and real-world Christ-following for the last almost thirty years helped us navigate the treacherous waters we faced on a daily basis.

To David, Paul, Chana, Jimmy, Bro. Dave, and Delynn, thank you for your wonderful input and encouragement. Your insight and advice helped to make this book as strong as it could be.

To Adam, our amazing editor, thank you for taking our rough edges and smoothing them out. You are possibly the most diversely well-read person we know. We are honored to have you involved with this project. But, in full disclosure, we still left some of those commas in place…

To Paul, Chris, Brent, Lance, and Tara, thank you for your help with the design and logistics of launching this book and our ministry. We are appreciative of you using your gifts to be a blessing to others. You have helped us become one's best "first glance" into our world.

To Dr. Robert Krance and all the other physicians, nurses, and support staff of Texas Children's Hospital, thank you for tirelessly serving our girl. Thank you, for not only doing your jobs, but doing them with excellence and personal care, as well. In our loneliest times, you became family. In our darkest hours, you became knowledge and light. Thank you for the hugs, listening to our frustrations, and for showing compassion. Katie definitely had her favorites (and you know who you are…).

To Dr. Ammar Morad and his team, along with the staff of Women's and Children's Hospital, we are grateful for the care you gave our Katie. Thank you for your expediency and guidance through what would become our greatest challenge.

To Valerie and the amazing folks at His Grace Foundation, for being a light in the darkness and a help to the helpless. You brought comfort and joy in a very special way, showing us what it truly means to walk in "His grace."

To Vicky, Marty and Anna, Alice, Sharon, Megan, Miranda, Jordy and Lindsay, Beau and Lauren, Shawn and Nichole, and a host of unnamed coaches, teachers, pastors, and all of you who made an impact on Katie, and helped mold who she became. Your contributions may have not been seen by many, but they were broadcast to the world as she walked through life's most difficult scenarios. Only eternity will tell the tale of how your wisdom and influence shaped our girl's world view. Every jewel in every one of her crowns is shared with you.

To all of our friends from all corners of the globe who supported us, not only through finances, but through prayer, during our journey, we sincerely thank you for letting God use you to become what the Church was always intended to be.

And especially, to all of our fellow bone marrow patient families at Texas Children's Hospital, the family we all never intended to have, but one we are so grateful to be in. Thank you for sharing your journey with us, as we shared ours with you.

CONTENTS

THE BACKSTORY

Daphne

I always thought our family led a pretty normal life. We were settled in a routine of work, school, church, extra-curricular activities, and regularly scheduled family nights. I loved what our family looked like.

I met my husband, Richard, in 1991, at a Burger King on the campus of USL (University of Southwestern Louisiana, now known as University of Louisiana at Lafayette). I was a brand-new Christian and had been invited by a friend to have lunch with her pastor and a group of Christ-following college kids. His line was, "Haven't I met you before?" My response was a stern, "No," and, as he says, "a very-much implied brush-off." I wasn't interested. I was in love with Jesus. He was the only man I needed. As the years went on, while I did have a couple of boyfriends, Richard wasn't one of them. In fact, I recall him being quite rude to me, just like the grade-school boy who'd pull a girl's hair as a sign of endearment. I still don't understand that kind of affection, but Richard had that act down.

Despite this fact, at some point through the years, we became friends. Then, one night after a

Sunday evening church service, he asked me to go out with him. I didn't know what to say because I really was only interested in a friendship, but I agreed, with the stipulation that it was an "only as friends" situation. That night at TGI Friday's, over spinach and artichoke dip, I realized he was much more than I had ever thought. I fell head over heels in love with this guy within a matter of weeks. But, if I'm being totally honest, I've never been more in love with him than I am today.

We were married on December 16, 1994. We moved from our hometown of Lafayette, Louisiana to Tulsa, Oklahoma, where I attended Oral Roberts University and Richard worked at Oral Roberts Television. The six years we lived in Tulsa were some of the best years of our lives. This was a town full of megachurches and ministries. We learned a lot about the inner workings of both, but also learned a lot about God. We both treasure the time we had there, but after our first child, Kylie, was born, we were ready to move back home to be closer to family and friends.

Finally, when I was eight months' pregnant with our second child and *enormous*, we loaded up a U-Haul, our dog, and a three-year-old Kylie, and headed home to Lafayette. That second child took a long time to finally make her arrival. The doctors had given us a due date of September 16, 2000. Two weeks after that date, she wasn't even budging. Carrying an overdue baby in south Louisiana heat is no joke. The doctor set a date to induce. And, in true form to who this child would be, after an overnight stay and induction in full force, she *still* didn't budge. When the doctor came in the next day at noon and said I was only dilated half a centimeter, I bawled my eyes out. How long can a baby stay in a mama? This was getting ridiculous. Something had to give. The doctor suggested a C-section and my oh-so-sympathetic husband asked how much that would cost. I

4

wanted to punch him in his frugal face. However, I didn't, and we decided to go home.

Yes, we went home after being induced and agreed to try again after another week. One week later, the night before I was scheduled for another induction, I went into labor. After 22 grueling hours, two of those just pushing, our Katie (Katherine Mackenzie) finally made her arrival, October 6, 2000. She had the loudest scream and cry of any baby I'd ever heard. In fact, the doctor asked me if I wanted him to put her back in. It was seriously ear-piercing. But her cries eventually stopped after she was placed in my arms, and we proceeded to fall even more in love with this baby girl. She came into this world a fighter and never backed down from anything she faced her entire life.

Richard became the media director at a large church in Lafayette, Louisiana (the very church we attended together before we were married). When Katie was almost three years old, I began teaching at a local Christian school. My two girls attended school where I taught. It was the perfect situation. At some point, I grew restless and knew God was moving me out of teaching and into something else. Eventually, I quit teaching and began working alongside my husband as a media production assistant. We made a great team and worked extremely well together. I worked with him for seven years before moving on to another place of employment. Little did I know at that time, that God was preparing us to work together in the most dire of situations for an extended period of time.

During my time at the church, I moved into the role of women's ministry director. I developed quite a passion for reaching the women of the church and beyond, encouraging them to take a more active role in their church and community. In addition, Richard and I were both worship leaders and highly involved with music and productions at the church. This was definitely a strong passion for each of us, as we always desired to see people worshipping God fully.

As you can imagine, our two girls lived at the church. It was their second home. They were there after school and during the summer; they attended every church event there was and were "all in" like their parents. Our girls grew and each developed their own gifts and talents in the way of music, each spending time on the worship teams. Kylie graduated from a performing arts high school and moved on to Hillsong College in Sydney, Australia. Katie was only able to sing for worship a couple times in the youth group before she was forced to give it up when her health became an issue.

At this point, our life was about to get wrecked … wrecked in the worst way I could have ever thought or imagined. I longed for normalcy again. A boring life would be even better. What did we do to ever deserve this? What did Katie do? Why us? Where was God? So many questions. So much pain. I came to realize that we would never understand any of it.

Katie wrote this song from her bed at Texas Children's Hospital, and it was the last time I'd ever hear her sing:

"Still Rising"

Inhale, hold my breath inside my chest
Lie awake at night, I can never get no rest
Waiting for a yes, take a guess, feel it coming up
I can hear the silence, can't believe it's just begun

It's one, it's two, I just want to see You
I'm suffocating, the walls are caving in

Losing my mind, losing sleep

Got my demons after me
It's just a phase, so hopefully
I'll find who I'm supposed to be

And through the night
I'm trying to fight, trying to fight for my life
When morning comes
Will I recognize who I've become

Exhale, so ready to unveil
Who I have become, singing like a nightingale
All my worries fail, I can tell that good has come my way
Looking out of the jail, now, I don't have to stay

It's three, it's four, open up the door
Let the light in, I'm not counting anymore

Losing my mind, losing sleep
Got my demons after me
It's just a phase, so hopefully
I'll find who I'm supposed to be

And through the night
I'm trying to fight, trying to fight for my life
When morning comes
Will I recognize who I've become

I'm still rising with the sun

This is her story.
This is our story.
We are still rising.

DIFFERENT
Richard

You were unsure which pain is worse - the shock of what
happened or the ache for what never will.
- Simon Van Booy, *Everything Beautiful Began After*

We knew this time would be different.

At 11:43 p.m., on Wednesday, July 19th, 2017, we got a call from Texas Children's Hospital. Normally, a call at that time would be from Katie, asking for sweet tea, or making sure we were going to bring her what she wanted to eat the next day, but this one was different. We hardly ever got calls from the hospital itself.

When Katie got admitted for the last time, on July 3rd, we felt it was different. We were used to the routine of being inpatient, her getting better, then going home, all while wishing this would be the last time the cycle occurred. In a way, our wish was granted, for, indeed, this was the last time this cycle occurred. It just wasn't in the way we had hoped.

The call was from the PICU doctor, telling us that Katie's blood pressure was continuing to drop, and her lactate levels had risen by an even wider margin than before. She feared there wasn't much time left. This surprised us as Katie had seemed to improve during the day. The second Daphne picked up the phone, she was in motion, getting dressed, getting ready to head to the hospital. She went into the living room and woke Kylie, to tell her what was happening. Kylie had flown in from Australia to see her sister and was sleeping on our tiny pullout couch in our temporary home located in an apartment complex in Houston's Medical Center. Daphne's parents had also arrived the previous day and were asleep in the extra bedroom. I got myself ready, and in a matter of minutes, Daphne and I were out the door of our apartment and on the road to the hospital. Kylie would follow with Daphne's parents about thirty minutes later.

At that time of night, the Texas Medical Center is a ghost town. Even the biggest, busiest medical center in the world experiences a lull in the middle of night's darkest hours. Our route down Holcombe Boulevard was peaceful, but with an eerie sense that this drive would be different. Daphne and I drove in silence. We suspected what we were about to face. We suspected that things were going to change. In a way, night's darkest hours were a metaphor of what would become ours.

We could never have prepared for what was ahead. We were about to say goodbye to the sweetest girl we'd ever met.

At this point, one might wonder why we weren't with her in her hospital room, and that wonder would be fully justified. The pediatric ICU (PICU) rooms at Texas Children's Hospital have no place for a parent to rest other than two extremely uncomfortable chairs and a waiting room that is as conducive to sleep as water is to fire. Katie had grown quite accustomed to us leaving for the night when she was in PICU, for she knew we needed sleep to be ready for the long days there with her. Plus, those incredible nurses turned many of her nights into mini spa sessions. When she was in a regular room, we swapped out nights, so that she always had someone with her. We even had regular "family sleepovers" at least twice a month.

As we walked into her room, we saw the familiar sight of our beautiful girl sleeping amidst a mountain of machines, pumps, tubes, monitors, and all the other things that accompany a critical-care patient. Katie had been intubated and on a ventilator since the previous Saturday. She was on continuous dialysis (CRRT), three pain meds, and the dreaded "three pressers." One of the nurses our family had grown quite close to had explained to Daphne the week prior that once a child hits three pressers (blood pressure medicines), it would be cause for great concern. We thought things were looking up since she had actually come off of one of the pressers the day before, but she was back on all three tonight.

She also said that she had seen kids with severe long-term illnesses hang on simply for their parents' sake, and that once their parents told them it was okay to let go and stop fighting, they felt like they had permission to do so. It usually wasn't much longer before the child passed. Our Katie had always been a fighter, always wanted to continue on, always wanted to beat this thing. She always felt like God was going to use her situation to speak to thousands, if not millions of people.

Bear in mind that we were not strangers to PICU. At this point, Katie had spent more than fourteen of the previous nineteen months in the hospital (almost eleven of those without leaving), and over six of those were spent in PICU, although not all at once. Her longest stretch was for a little over two months, from April to July, 2016. She had been on and off a ventilator at least ten times, and at least six times on and off CRRT. We had gotten used to the fast-paced atmosphere, although, at night, things did slow down a little.

But, again, this time was different.

13

There was a look of grave concern on the nurse's face, combined with an almost pity-like expression towards us. We saw it in the three PICU doctors' faces as well, and in others who happened to be around. It was as if the entire staff knew what was coming. They'd seen this scenario play out many times. Actually, to a lesser extent, we had seen it play out as well, except from a distance. In our time in the PICU, six families had gone home without their child.

We would be Number Seven.

We each took turns holding her hand, sitting beside her in, crying silent tears, still praying for a miracle, wishing things were different. When Kylie arrived, she joined in with us. Very few words were spoken that night, until two of Katie's PICU doctors came in to let us know our options.

"Our unit is very good at keeping kids alive until the family is ready," said one of them.

I wasn't exactly ready to hear a sentence like that. No parent is.

He continued, "Of course, Katie is different. She's quite resilient, and things could change, but my professional opinion is that we could keep her on the ventilator and we'd be right here again tomorrow, having this same conversation."

At this point, Katie was on the ventilator's highest setting, and we were bumping up on the highest amount of blood pressure medicine allowed. There simply was nowhere else to go. "When you are ready to discuss your options, let me know."

And then, he said something I'll never forget. "I just want you guys to know that I'm a believer, and I know you are as well. It's obvious to all of us that you are people of faith. My daughters pray for my patients every night, and they have been praying for Katie for over a year."

Those words, in that moment, were a comfort to us like nothing we could have imagined. It was such a great source of peace to us to have this particular doctor this evening, a fellow Christ-follower with us, knowing that, barring a miracle, our daughter was about to go home to be with Jesus. But what gave us the most peace was the conversation we'd had with Katie just four days prior.

The previous Sunday was the first time Katie went on three pressers. With that in mind, coupled with the conversation Daphne had with her nurse, we knew it was time to have a serious conversation with Katie and start to make plans to fly Kylie in. One of the PICU doctors actually told us that in her opinion, bringing Kylie in was the right thing to do, for two reasons: first, Kylie's arrival might just give Katie the bump she needed to get over all the issues with which she was dealing, and second, it would be unfair to Kylie for us to wait until it was too late for her to see her sister if this were "it" for Katie.

Once Kylie's flight was booked, then came the hard conversation we never thought we'd have to have, but one both of us had already played out several times in each of our minds. We stood on either side of her, Daphne on her left and me on her right. Katie laid there, eyes closed, labored breathing with the ventilator, intubated. Her nurse had just informed us that Katie was about to go on a paralytic med so that her body wouldn't have to work at breathing, giving her more strength to fight off yet another unknown infection. Her nurse actually backed off on the pain meds a bit so that she could better communicate with us.

"Hey, baby. It's Daddy. Mommy is right there, holding your left hand, and Kylie is on her way from Australia. Squeeze your mommy's hand if you can hear me."

A squeeze in the affirmative meant she knew we were there, and she understood us.

I went on. "Katie, we know you're tired. We know you have fought hard, and we know you have done the very best you can, and you've been so amazing. We want you to know that we are so proud of you."

Daphne continued, "Baby, if you still want to fight, we will fight with you. But if you are tired, if you are done fighting, we understand. Please don't think you are letting us down if you're done with the fight. Do you understand what I'm saying?"

Another squeeze, signaling her cognizance.

"Katie, do you really understand what it is we are saying, and what that means for you, and where you will be?" I asked. "If you know what it is we are saying, bat your eyelids at me."

She batted her eyelids, never opening her eyes.

We cried over her, held her, prayed with her, and watched her go back to sleep as her nurse increased her pain meds.

A little while later, Daphne decided to go back to the apartment to shower and change, because she had already been there all day, and we decided we'd stay the night, together with our girl. After Daphne left, I tried to talk to Katie again. Her nurse saw the failed exchange and backed off the pain meds so Katie could communicate. I wanted to be sure Katie knew exactly what we had asked her, and, like many times before, I *needed* to know what was on her mind.

"Hey, sweet girl. It's Daddy. If you hear me, squeeze my hand."

Hand squeezed.

"Do you remember our conversation a little while ago?"

Another hand squeeze.

"Do you remember what we talked about?"

Squeeze.

"Katie, this is really serious, and I want to be sure you understood what it is, exactly, we were saying. Did you understand what you giving up really means?"

Yet again, another squeeze.

Wanting to make sure I knew she knew what we were talking about, I phrased my question in a different way, so that there would be no mistaking the meaning, for both of us.

"Katie, are you ready to stop fighting and just go be with Jesus?"

At that moment, instead of squeezing my hand, she opened her eyes, looked at me straight in the face, looked up at the ceiling, and nodded her head. As sad as it made me feel, and as much as I knew I was going to miss this incredible young woman, I knew she was ready to enter into her eternal rest and reward. She was ready to be with the One she loved more than her own life, the One with whom she most identified, for it was His suffering that made her suffering more bearable.

After the PICU doctor offered his comforting words, he left the room, leaving Daphne, Kylie, and me alone with Katie to determine what would happen next. This was agonizing. How could we make such a decision? We discussed a few options and decided we would remove the machines. We stepped out of the room so Daphne's parents could come in and say their goodbyes. Obviously, they were heartbroken, but they knew we were making the right decision.

Once they left, we spoke with the doctor about how things would progress. The first to come off would be the continuous dialysis machine (CRRT), then the blood pressure meds. At first, I didn't want to take her off of the ventilator, because the doctor told us that extubation can be "ugly," and I really didn't want my last memories of Katie to have that imagery in them. Shortly after making that call, Daphne asked me to reconsider (it was more like a much-needed scolding, to be honest), stating that Katie hated the breathing tube, and that she was always in such a hurry to take it out, every single time she went on that ventilator. She really loathed it. I realized my selfishness, and agreed that the tube should come out.

One by one, the machines were disconnected. As a last act of faith, maybe as a last act of desperation, as I stood in the corner of the room, watching the nurses do their work, watching my sweet Katie lay there, I kept telling God that He could still work a miracle. I begged Him to do just that.

Dialysis machine disconnected and turned off.

"God, You can still work a miracle. It's not too late. I trust You."

Blood transfusion, anti-viral meds, anti-fungal meds, hydrocortisone, antibiotics all disconnected and their pumps turned off.

"God, You can still work a miracle. It's not too late. I trust You."

Blood pressure meds disconnected and their pumps turned off.

"God, You can still work a miracle. It's not too late. I trust You."

Tube pulled. Ventilator turned off.

"God, You can still work a miracle. It's not too late. I trust You."

Katie was disconnected from everything but her pain meds, so that her passing would be as peaceful as possible. Once everything was removed, I noticed how helpless and baby-like she was. We all huddled around her, holding her hands, cuddling up as close as we possibly could. She took a breath every five seconds or so, but the doctor assured us her heart was still beating.

In that moment, I remembered how Katie would never want to go to bed without praying. Even at sixteen years old, just as a little child would, she always expected bedtime prayers. I gathered our family around her and we held hands and prayed one final bedtime prayer together. When it was over, I looked up at the doctor, stethoscope in hand, the same doctor who so eloquently expressed his faith in Christ earlier, listening to her heart.

"Her heartbeat is still there, but very faint."

A couple more breaths, five or six seconds apart.

More tears, more hugs, more of us telling her how much we loved her, how incredibly proud we were of her, and how amazing she was, more watching of my baby girl slip into eternity.

And with one more listen with the stethoscope, at 4:59 a.m., on Thursday, July 20th, 2017, we heard the doctor utter the words we never wanted to hear. But in that moment, they strangely brought comfort.

"She's with our Lord."

As the stream of nurses, assistants, doctors, and even janitorial staff came through to bid Katie a final farewell, we were, yet again, overcome by the thought of just how many lives our little girl touched. Not only our Louisiana family and friends, but also our new family at Texas Children's Hospital, as well as extended family all over the world. Even her doctor, who has seen it all, upon entering the room, had obviously been crying, and still had fresh tears in his eyes. We were later told that he had been "mopey" all day. One of her favorite nurses stated, "Everyone has a Katie story." And it was so true. This one truly was different. One meeting with this girl and your world was different. As a good friend of mine once put it, "You didn't just meet Katie. You *experienced* Katie."

As we returned to our apartment, roughly five hours after Katie's passing, Kylie went ahead of us into the building. I stopped Daphne on the curb, pulled her close to me, and asked her one simple question.

"Do you have any regrets?"

"None. Do you?"

"None."

We had some sense of peace that day, not only because we knew Katie was no longer in pain, not only because we knew where she was, and is today, and will be forevermore, but also because we gave it everything we had. But we were not the ones who had the original idea of living our lives with no regrets. She, too, gave it everything she had. That's how she lived her entire life. We learned it from her, our amazing Katie Mac. Because of her, our world was different.

THIS GIRL, PART ONE
Daphne

She was one of the rare ones, so effortlessly herself, and
the world loved her for it.
- Harper Lee, *To Kill a Mockingbird*

As I mentioned earlier, Katie came into this world as a force to be reckoned with, and that continued for the rest of her life.

The crazy thing is that, as a baby, she was attached to me. Separation anxiety is a real thing, and Katie had it immensely. I didn't understand it. I had followed the same baby "rules" I had followed with Kylie (who slept in her own bed within two weeks of being born, and through the night by two months). Eventually, I realized those rules and books don't work for every baby and I just winged it. I was too darn exhausted so I ignored what the books said about letting her sleep with me. I ignored what they said about letting her cry it out because, after four hours, Richard and I couldn't take it anymore. Katie showed us that we were going to be doing this baby thing *her* way.

All she wanted was me... me, me, me, 24/7. I longed for breaks from having this baby on my hip. I looked forward to my weekly trips to Target, which, as all women know, could turn into a three-hour venture. I walked aimlessly through those aisles, Starbucks in hand, cherishing each moment before I'd have to return home. Don't get me wrong; I loved this baby girl with all my heart. But any moms whose children have suffered from extreme separation anxiety know what I'm talking about. I just had to take a break sometimes. The sad part was that for those three hours that I was gone, Richard tried everything he could to comfort Katie. Nothing would work. She would cry the entire time I was gone and, yes, that could be three hours. And then, when I showed up back at home, all was right with this baby's world.

Leaving her in the nursery at church would rip my heart out. I left her crying every single time. However, over time, Katie grew to love the nursery director and, as long as I left her in her hands, she more easily coped with the separation. Thank God! Mama needed church, too.

Those months seemed to last forever. I couldn't wait until she grew out of it. And, then, one day, the tide turned. Katie became the most independent toddler I'd ever seen. In fact, Richard once went to pick her up from the nursery one morning after church service and noticed that the two other babies in the nursery with her were crying. Our sweet Katie was walking around with a pacifier in her mouth and one pacifier in each of her hands. She had turned from a crying baby who only wanted her mama into a gangster baby who stole pacifiers and toys from the other babies!

Fast forward to age three, when her personality truly began to shine. From the time Katie could first talk, she made us laugh. She was always naturally funny and full of energy. One of her preschool teachers said it best: "Katie is one hundred percent all the time. If she's going to be bad, she's one hundred percent bad, but if she's going to be good, she's one hundred percent good. Let's hope we can harness all this for good." She was so right. There was no middle ground with Katie, ever. She was one hundred percent, all in, all the way, all the time, even if you didn't want her to be.

Katie turned out to be an incredible athlete, even at a young age. She played soccer from the time she was six years old until eighth grade. In fact, Katie had just made her junior high school's soccer team right before her diagnosis. She was so excited to be able to play her first game for them, but never made it that far. All through her years of playing soccer, she was known as the very aggressive player. She hated losing and was all in on the soccer field, just like she was in life.

One particular season, Katie's coach made her an alternate for goalie. She hated it. She was always right in the thick of the game as a sweeper or forward. But, what he said made sense: "All the other girls turn their heads when the ball is coming to them, but Katie looks straight at it before she dives to stop it." This same coach screamed from the sidelines, "Take her out, Katie," in reference to another player, which, in hindsight, probably wasn't the best coaching advice. However, he knew Katie would go for it and, unfortunately, for some of the other girls, they were on the receiving end of Katie's brute force when her eyes were set on getting that ball. I even got called into the principal's office at Katie's elementary school one year because she hurt a boy while playing ball during recess. My response was that, when you're playing ball with Katie, you should know what you're in for, and also, don't be such a wuss.

Katie also loved to sing. Kylie was and naturally talented when it comes to music. She has an amazing voice, but also plays many instruments and is a great songwriter. Katie always looked up to her older sister and wanted to learn how to sing harmony and play guitar. She had a passion for worship, just like the rest of her family, and wanted to sing on the worship team. When she asked me how to sing harmony, I began to show her simply by picking out harmony parts to songs on the radio. I would have her sing with me, and, at times, have her try to pick parts out. We would do this any time we were in the car together. She did the same with her daddy.

Over time, we would hear her singing for hours on end up in her room, picking out harmonies on her own. What came naturally to her sister didn't come so easily to her, but she always worked at it. She was determined, and she never gave up. Eventually, she could pick out parts on her own and began singing with the youth worship team. She also, with her sister's and daddy's help, learned guitar chords and would spend much time working on or playing her favorite One Direction songs before eventually writing her own songs.

One summer, Katie came home from one of the many youth camps she would attend and announced, "Mama, I know what God wants me to do."

I was taken aback and asked, "What's that, baby?"

She'd had an encounter with the Lord. She responded, "God wants me to reach my school for Him."

And just like that, a vision was born. Katie had always gone to a private Christian school and was heading off to a public junior high school for the first time, so this was going to be different. That fall, she did it. She made flyers for a prayer meeting. She forced me to buy doughnuts and milk, thinking that would be a lure for kids to come (which, of course, it was). I attended that first meeting. She and a friend led a short devotional and asked for prayer requests. They prayed and Katie invited kids to come to her church youth group services. Her daddy and I were so proud. That's a hard thing for a kid to do.

One of her teachers described Katie as "tenacious." It was such a perfect word for her. Once

Katie got something in her head, she never let go of it. Her tenacity is part of the reason she made it as far as she did the last few years of her life. She was tenacious to the end.

Her tenacity paled in comparison to her selfless heart. Not only was this visible during Katie's treatment, but even before her diagnosis. After she was diagnosed, her selflessness showed even more, because she had every right to be selfish. She relayed a story to me once as we made our way home from just another routine evening emergency room visit. A boy had asked her to go with him to the 8th grade dance and she'd said the exact same thing I'd said to her daddy when he asked me out over twenty-three years earlier: "Just as friends, right?" It worked out for her father, but it didn't for this boy.

The boy explained that he didn't want to go just as friends; he wanted to go as a real date. To which she responded, "I'm not interested in having a relationship right now." She then went into a lengthy explanation why she wasn't interested in relationships at this time in her life. I giggled as she briefed me on the story. Good girl. But the best part was when she told the boy he should ask one of her friends to go with him because she didn't have a date. Who does that? This truly unselfish, compassionate girl.

When Kylie graduated from high school, we were just in the beginning stages of this journey with Katie. We worked as hard as we could to make graduation day a happy, glorious one for Kylie, celebrating all her accomplishments. It was sad when we realized Katie wouldn't be able to attend the graduation ceremony because of the huge crowd that would be in the arena. But she went on with the day as normally as she could. As night fell, family and visitors left and it was just our little family at home, in the quiet. I donned my surgical gloves, gathered up my supplies, and began to flush Katie's PICC line, as I did every night. But this time, Katie wore a serious, sad face. When I asked what was wrong, she began to cry. I prodded her to tell me what was going on.

Through tears, she said, "I just don't feel like myself." I knew she was tired. I knew it had been a long day, especially since we had just gotten home from a *lengthy* fifteen-hour doctor's appointment/hospital visit at one o'clock that same morning. She was emotional and hadn't been her typical, lively self that day. She said, "I hate that I couldn't really be a part of Kylie's special day like I wanted to. I hate that all of you have to worry about me and my situation when it's *her* day." In that moment, I saw her heart. She hated what this was doing to *us* more than to her. She was worried about us, not about herself. This part of her personality only shone more as her sickness grew.

She always amazed the doctors and nurses with how she would pull through each life-threatening situation after another. They truly thought she was the one who'd make it through this. That's what we thought, too. One of the doctors said, "Katie has this amazing reserve and resilience that we can't ever predict." She was definitely unpredictable in the way of her medical prognoses. Numerous times, nurses referred to her as "the strongest girl we know." She overcame so many obstacles. I watched this girl go from being bedridden, not even being able to sit up on her own, to pushing through unimaginable, intense pain and, not only sitting up, but also walking again.

She was and will always be my hero. I'm reminded of how much she fought every time I was facing some sort of struggle. The struggles I had were nothing compared to what she fought against. I never imagined my own daughter would teach her mom so much about courage and strength. I am forever changed.

But, more than that, I am forever grateful to God for letting me be her mom.

HOW DID WE GET HERE?
Daphne

We can make our plans, but the Lord determines our steps.
- Proverbs 16:9 (NLT)

The first days into this journey seemed like a blur. I hate using the word "journey," but there doesn't seem to be a more appropriate word. To me, a journey sounds wonderful. It sounds like an amazing vacation, like backpacking through Europe or an African safari. It sounds like something good. But I can tell you: not all journeys feel good.

This one felt like pure hell.

Even today, it still feels like hell. As one of Katie's doctors told us, after I questioned whether Katie could be suffering from PTSD (Post-Traumatic Stress Disorder), "It's not the kids who have PTSD, it's the parents." I can honestly say that the memories still haunt us.

Granted, I know we're not the only people in the world who've lost someone. We're not the only people in the world who've lost a child after a lengthy illness. There are parents who've journeyed through illness much longer than we have. So it's safe to say that there are a lot of people out there who are living lives that feel like hell. This is just our story.

It was Easter 2015. Katie had started to show signs of being sick before then, but we wouldn't discover that until later. Being the extremely active child that she was, a few extra bruises were not uncommon. She always had bruises. She was an aggressive volleyball and soccer player. In fact, she was aggressive in everything she did. However, bruises began to show up in odd places, and with no explanation of how or why they were there. And these weren't your run-of-the-mill bruises; these things were enormous.

One evening, Katie hurried down the stairs to show me a particular bruise on her arm. It was dark blue and the size of a baseball, maybe larger. I asked her what in the world she had done to cause such a large bruise. She didn't have a clue and said she was just sitting on her bed. Of course, I didn't believe her and assumed she was doing something she probably wasn't supposed to have been doing, like jumping from her bed to the floor or working on her unique dance moves. Like I said, this girl was rough and tough and always active. Never still.

As the weeks went on, more large bruises appeared. But she was playing soccer and was exceptionally active during recess or any other time there was a ball in play. Soon the bruises were accompanied by broken blood vessels (purpura), which showed up as tiny, pinpoint, red dots on different areas of her skin. At this point, I called this to the attention of my mom. She's a nurse and I've always run all our family's health issues by her first, from warts to head colds.

On Easter Day, 2015, Katie wore her new, precious, navy blue, floral print, sleeveless dress, and her bruises were more noticeable than ever. We joked that someone at church was going to call child protective services on us because she looked abused. As I look back at the pictures from that day, I can see how tired she looked. There was definitely an exhaustion in her eyes that said something was up.

Her fatigue became more noticeable, but this is often normal for a teenager. She was tired all the time. On the weekends, she would sleep until afternoon and still nap. During the school week, she was even more exhausted. But, again, this seemed like normal teenage behavior. Sleeping was my main hobby when I was that age. No major warning signs there.

When we arrived at my parents' house for Easter lunch, my mom assessed Katie's bruised areas and told me I should take her to the doctor to get some blood work done. Wow. Was she ever right!

Although Katie had all these bruises and was tired, she still acted like her normal self. She was still active, still funny, and mostly felt fine. This girl had never been sick her whole life. I called her my "healthy child" because her sister had been quite sickly as a child. Katie's claim to fame was that she had only vomited once in her lifetime before all this happened. Oh how things would change.

We got in quickly with a doctor who didn't seem to think this was too much to be worried about, but ordered blood tests just to be safe. He examined her and, knowing how active she was, told me it was probably nothing. After all, Katie was acting totally normal. No real symptoms other than the bruising. No rush to get the labs done that day. We would wait a few days when Richard or I could leave work and take her in for the tests.

However, by the weekend, Katie informed me that she had been on her cycle for two weeks. I understand about irregular periods in teenagers, but this didn't seem right. That's when I got a little worried. Richard took her at 8:00 on a Monday morning to get her labs done. They were the first ones there, so they were seen quickly and Richard checked Katie into school afterward.

About an hour later, I received a phone call from the doctor. He told me to get over to the school immediately, pick Katie up, and take her to the emergency room. Her platelet count was a 5, which meant nothing to me at the time. Little did I know that I would become way too familiar with platelets, blood, and all kinds of medical terms and procedures.

Platelets give your blood the ability to clot, which also explained why Katie's cycle had not stopped. The doctor said, "She could fall and scrape her knee and bleed to death." Thank God I only worked about five minutes from her school! I frantically rushed over to the school and had them call her to the front office. I can still picture the surprise on her face as she walked into the office with her backpack and work for the rest of the day. She said, "I didn't know you were coming to pick me up. I was just starting math class." I braced myself to tell her where we were headed and calmly informed her that it was just for tests and, again, was nothing to be worried about. I always tried to keep her calm, but I could immediately tell that she was nervous and anxious. We were soon in the emergency room, where we would stay for the entire day, until we were admitted to the hospital late in the afternoon.

Katie always had a fear of needles but that day she was stuck multiple times for more blood draws, more tests, and then the dreaded IV, which took many attempts to get in. By the end of the stay, her fear of needles seemed to dissipate.

She was admitted because her platelets were so low she needed a platelet transfusion. However, her red blood cell count and white blood cell count were also low. The blood tests could only tell us so much so we would have to wait until the next day for more detailed results.

Katie received transfusions throughout the night. The doctor came in the next morning and told us the blood tests were inconclusive so he would have to get the results he needed from a bone marrow biopsy.

"When you look at the bone marrow, it's like looking into the future," he said. "What happens in the bone marrow, the building blocks of the blood, will eventually happen in the blood."

Our minds spun. What does all this mean? Katie felt fine. She felt well.

We questioned him on what could be happening, never imagining the possibilities he would give us. What would he be looking for in the bone marrow? There were three things that could be causing Katie's condition, presenting itself in the bone marrow's inability to make blood cells: a viral infection, aplastic anemia, or leukemia.

That last word was shocking. "Leukemia." It's a word no one is ever prepared to hear. When Katie heard "leukemia," she got extremely quiet, as we all did. Once the doctor and nurses left the room, she looked up at me and said, "Cancer?" and began to cry. I cuddled up in the bed next to her, held her, and cried with her. Richard began to cry. We were a complete mess.

I wish I could tell you we weren't. I wish I could tell you this news didn't phase us because of what strong Christians we are. But I can't. The uncertainty made us anxious and we had to push though the fear that would continuously loom over us, not just in this moment, but also in many scary moments to come.

Through our cries and in the midst of our fear, we began to speak truth to Katie and to ourselves. The truth is that God is a healer. God is good. God loves us. God didn't want Katie to be sick. God still had great plans for her, just like we had told her all her life. We prayed and believed and hoped for the best. Our faith grew as we quoted Scripture to her. We knew God would work this out for us. He had already been so faithful in our lives. Countless people came and prayed for her. We continued to hold on to hope.

We did literally everything we knew to do. All we could do was wait and trust God. This is the point where faith is tested. I continued to ask myself, "Do you believe God is who He says He is? Do you believe God will do what He says He will do? Now's the time to exercise your faith. You can't just believe it when life is going great. It doesn't work like that."

I stayed with Katie that night for the first of many sleepless hospital nights.

The next morning, the test was over pretty quickly, and the doctor immediately checked the labs before sending them off to the pathologists. He gave us a preliminary diagnosis of aplastic anemia. We were extremely grateful it was not leukemia and continued to pray for an even better report after the final labs came back. I, of course, began to research aplastic anemia, since I had never heard of it. It seemed like no one had ever heard of it. In fact, our doctor, who has treated hundreds of leukemia patients, had seen only one other aplastic anemia patient in our area of the country. It's a pretty rare disease. Only one to two people per million per year are diagnosed with aplastic anemia. That's about 300-600 cases a year in the U.S.

Aplastic anemia is a disease where the bone marrow stops making enough red blood cells, white blood cells, and platelets for the body. Any blood cells the marrow manages to make are normal, but there just aren't enough of them. So while we were thankful it was not leukemia, this was still not a good diagnosis.

Because Katie had received another platelet transfusion, her counts were good enough to go home the day after her procedure. The doctor was convinced it was aplastic anemia and told us to start thinking about how we wanted to treat it. We would meet with him after he took a day to extensively study all of Katie's lab work. Katie was able to go back to school the next day and perform in a theatre production. The next few days, she complained of headaches (another sign of anemia), but seemed to be okay for the most part.

We met with the doctor the following week and he confirmed his original diagnosis. Katie had more blood drawn to show her levels. Her headaches were due to the fact that, in addition to her low platelets, her red blood cell count was low and she was very anemic. She would need to be seen frequently for blood transfusions in the weeks ahead. We would have to keep an eye on her, almost like when she was a baby. I actually checked in on her one early morning to make sure she was still breathing, like I used to do when she was a newborn. Yes, I was one of those moms.

On the next office visit, we had an extensive discussion with the doctor about treatment. He was so patient with us, answered my barrage of questions, took his time, and explained everything in detail. The best treatment possible was a stem cell (bone marrow) transplant, which is what we had opted for at the beginning. Our doctor contacted Texas Children's Hospital (the hospital we had chosen after much research on our part) to discuss how they'd like to proceed. Since immediate family is always tested first, Richard, Kylie, and I were praying one of us would be a match. If one of us was not a match, the doctors would search the donor database for a match there. If no matches were found, there was a second option of immunosuppressive therapy as treatment. But we believed there was a match for Katie.

In the days that would follow, we waited. Watched and waited. At this point, I believed that waiting was the hardest part. I don't feel that way today. There were much harder parts to come. Yes, waiting sucks. But there are worse things out there. I'd gladly wait on test results or wait for sickness to get better or wait for pretty much anything nowadays. Waiting doesn't seem so bad, but more about that later on.

This was my journal entry after we received Katie's diagnosis:

> *This mama has a broken heart. I know my God is bigger than any disease or any sickness or any circumstance that would come our way. But watching your baby go through something like this is gut-wrenching.*
>
> *So, what do I do in the meantime? I pray. I cry. I talk.*
>
> *I spend most of the days just taking my thoughts captive. Our minds can go places they were never meant to go. As a thought comes into my mind, I may or may not start to tear up. I have to immediately cast that thought down, ask God to renew my mind, and begin to speak the truth that I know about God, who He is, and what He wants for us. It's all good.*
>
> *I've gotten onto this roller coaster of emotions and events, and I'm longing for the day that I can get off. It's coming, I know. But, right now, I just went down that first drop and I'm scared and holding on for dear life. I know that God is on our side and He's with us always. At the same time, I feel scared, I can feel peace because I know again, He is... well, just HE IS... He is everything I need, everything my family needs, and everything Katie needs.*

I filled our house with worship music. There was one song in particular that I had on repeat, Darlene Zschech's "In Jesus' Name." Katie began to sing the lyrics with me. We were proclaiming that Jesus' name is above any name, and that included the name of "aplastic anemia":

God is fighting for us,
God is on our side,
He has overcome, yes, He has overcome

We will not be shaken,
We will not be moved,
Jesus, You are here.

I will live, I will not die,
I will declare and lift You high,
Christ revealed and I am healed in Jesus' name.

I was doing everything I knew a good Christian should do. I was praying. I was believing. I was "speaking the Word over our situation." I was rebuking the enemy. I was filling us up with the Word of God, which says God is a healer. I believed it. We all did, and I tried desperately not to let anything sway my faith in a loving Father, whom I knew personally. I felt like I was always His girl. My family was His family. He would definitely work on our behalf, on Katie's behalf.

As we waited, trusted, and believed for Katie's healing, we tried to be as normal as possible in between doctor's visits, transfusions, and procedures.

Katie had to get a PICC (peripherally inserted central catheter) line. After so many pokes and transfusions, her veins were collapsing and this line would allow her to not have to go through multiple

41

attempts at getting needles in every week. A PICC line lasts for up to 6 months, making it easier to give her blood or medicine.

When the nurse called me about the PICC line and explained what it was, I quickly tried to get off the phone, telling her I'd have to discuss it with my husband. But I really just needed to get off the phone because I was starting to cry.

The words "more permanent" and the explanation of how the line would end near her heart made me lose my breath. I couldn't breathe. My heart ached and tears filled my eyes.

I wanted to scream, "No!" I don't want anything like this even close to permanent for my child. I was angry. I cried. Alone in my bedroom, I cried. I did not want this for my child at all. I could have dealt with this a lot better if it had been me and not her.

Once again, I got on my knees and prayed like I did every time I started to lose it. I prayed again that God would heal her. I prayed for a miracle. I prayed that God would renew my mind so that I could always trust and never doubt. I prayed that God would do what He's promised in His Word. I reminded myself, yet again, that God is a good Father. The BEST! What good Father doesn't want the best for His child? A good Father who loves my child even more than I do definitely wants the best for my child, His daughter.

These are the prayers I prayed throughout the day because I had to. It was the only way I could make it through the day.

In addition, I continued to immerse myself in worship music. It really does change the atmosphere wherever you are and helps with whatever you are going through. I didn't only need my atmosphere changed, I needed my mind changed and my circumstances changed.

We spent hours, sometimes entire days, at the doctor's office. I would sit next to my baby girl and pray, and those prayers consisted mostly of, "Jesus, I need you." Because, sometimes that was, literally, all I could say. I felt like a broken record: same thing, over and over every day. He *had* to hear me.

For the rest of the weeks to follow, I could only take each day as it came. I couldn't look ahead. I just couldn't. I couldn't make plans. I couldn't schedule anything. I didn't know what would be happening the next week or even what the end of the week would hold. I just didn't know anything. I was zombie-ish. I felt as numb, broken, and bruised as my daughter.

The only thing I knew was that my number-one priority was getting my baby girl well. That's it. That took precedence over everything.

There were other things on my mind. Our family had a lot going on—Kylie's high school graduation, her graduation party, putting our house on the market to sell, making sure it was totally ready to be put on the market to sell, getting it sold quickly, my new position at work, the things I needed to do at work in this new position, and then there was the whole moving once the house was sold… the list went on.

But, it was hard to think about those things when that one thing consumed my mind. So, I prayed… and prayed again… and prayed, "Jesus, help me."

Katie's PICC line was in and she began to get weekly rounds of platelets and red blood cell transfusions. Our days became consumed with doctor's office visits. Some days we arrived at 9:00 a.m. and didn't leave until close to 5:00 p.m. They were long days.

Very long days. Let's not forget that Richard and I were still trying to work full-time. Thank God our employers were very understanding.

I had many long conversations with Katie's doctor. I often thought his brain would explode from the large number of questions I asked him, but it didn't. He continued to be ever so patient with me and answered every question he could. We all grew to love him and were thankful for him. He was a smartie, definitely what you want in your child's doctor.

I, of course, was ready to get the ball rolling on the transplant process. Patience was never my strong suit. Unfortunately, my urgency as a mother was not felt among everyone else who saw this kind of stuff all day long. So, we waited more. We waited on phone calls from Texas Children's Hospital about everything: insurance, procedures, and most importantly, our testing to see if we could be her stem cell donor.

After yet another lengthy discussion with Katie's doctor, we made a slight change in our plans as far as treatment for her. The first plan and best option was one of us (Richard, Kylie, or myself) being a perfect stem cell donor match for Katie. It would be a 100% success rate/cure rate with a perfect match from her immediate family. However, once we started looking at an unrelated match, the success rate dropped to 75%.

Because of that percentage, we opted for immune therapy if none of us was a match for Katie, because that success rate/cure rate was 80%, which pushed it up to second place. We would look to the unrelated donor only as our third option, which we were praying we wouldn't even have to consider. That's where we were for weeks. We sat and waited for the phone to ring.

On one of those visits with the doctor, he had more bad news for Katie. The doctor informed Katie that, since her risk of infection was so high, she could not be in crowded places or even around a lot of people unless she wore a face mask. This was pretty devastating news for a 14-year-old girl. We had already been forced to pull Katie out of school, and she was finishing up the rest of the year as a homebound student. Of course, she hated that because she was such a social butterfly, but since it was close to the end of the year, maybe it was not so bad. But now, even church was iffy. We did grab lots of masks on the way out of the office that day and decided we would play it by ear. Otherwise she was home indefinitely. Maybe a run to the store or a less populated place would be possible, but not the mall on a Saturday unless she wore a mask. Who wants to wear a mask everywhere they go? It basically screams, "I am sick." No teenage girl I know would want to do this.

With this new restriction, Katie became somewhat depressed, pretty angry, and simply sad about the whole situation. All understandable. I just cried more. No matter how much I tried not to cry, I still did. This mama could not get it together. And if Katie was sad, I was more sad.

Katie finally said, "If anyone should be crying it should be me."

I laughed through my tears, and said, "I'm crying because I hate this for you and you're my baby girl. That's all."

Actually, she didn't cry very much at all. In fact, at the beginning of her illness, I can count on one hand the amount of tears I saw from her. I was pretty amazed at her strength and how brave she seemed.

She couldn't care less about the procedures, needles, blood, or any of the scary stuff. She only cared about not being able to do the same things all of her friends were doing. I told her it was only temporary, but that didn't appease her. I had full confidence this would be something that would be fixed, her healing all wrapped up in a neat little bow. Because that's how it's supposed to be for us as believers, right?

———————— ◯ ————————

As we waited for that call from Texas Children's Hospital, we tried to act normal. Of course, Richard and I were like ships in the night at this point. We were both consumed with all the things going on in our lives, everything happening at the same time. There was no alone time. No date nights. None of that stuff. Honestly, that kind of thing was the farthest thing from our minds. We barely had any moments alone at all. And, if we were alone, we were exhausted and asleep.

The morning I finally got the phone call from Texas Children's Hospital, I sent Richard off to work after a kiss, a hug, and an apology for throwing his good shoes in the garage sale pile. Our stress level was off the charts, and such an incident had sent him into a nervous breakdown. I assured him with full confidence, that we'd have a few minutes alone soon. Funny, I don't think that alone time ever happened that first year and it was few and far between much later on.

The nurse on the other end of the line gave me all the details of what to expect at our visit the following Monday. As we waited for this visit, we led our new normal life of doctor visits, infusions, using massive amounts of hand sanitizer, and creating social protective barriers around Katie wherever she went.

Everyone would ask how we were doing. What a loaded question. I don't think anyone ever really wanted me to get into it, so I always said, "Good." Were we "good"? As good as anyone would be in this type of scenario. I can see how God was sustaining us through it all. But, our family ran through the gamut of emotions on any given day: the good, the bad, the ugly.

———————————— ◯ ————————————

Our family finally made the three-hour trip to Houston for our much-anticipated visit to Texas Children's Hospital for testing and initial appointments with the doctors there.

It was surreal sitting in the waiting rooms with countless numbers of precious bald-headed babies and many other children in masks and wheelchairs. My heart was saddened. Not just saddened for my own child to have to go through something like this, but for all those children who were enduring sickness when they should have been concerned about playing and enjoying their friends. It broke my heart. It has to break the heart of God. If He is that good, good Father, He loves all these babies and wants each of them to be well.

We were at the hospital all day, meeting first with the hematologist and then the transplant doctor. There were extensive discussions, and the hematologist took more blood for more tests. The bit of news I had not yet heard was that aplastic anemia has a cause. It doesn't just appear; something triggers it. But all the tests for what could have caused it came back negative. So we didn't have a cause. Our doctors decided to look at some different genetic things through more testing. The hematologist ordered more blood drawn and wanted another sample from Katie's bone marrow, so another biopsy was put on the schedule for the following week. Basically, the doctor needed to rule out everything that could have been an underlying condition or cause for the aplastic anemia because this could also affect the way it would be treated.

When the doctor said that her diagnosis qualified Katie for Make-A-Wish, it struck me a little hard. Isn't Make-a-Wish for dying kids? I felt something rise up in me. My kid's *not* dying, lady. I felt my face get hot. But she explained that the foundation was not just for children who were dying, but also children who have a diagnosis which requires lots of treatment and extended hospital stays. That made me feel a little better. Of course, Katie was thrilled about that part. Finally, something she could be happy about.

We met with the transplant doctor in the afternoon. He examined Katie and we all got our blood drawn to be tested for a match for our sweet girl.

We learned that parents are not usually a match for their child, but there are instances where they have been. We each are half-matched, which means half of what Katie needed matched each of us. That's why a sibling is the best match for something like this because they get the same type of antigens (HLA - Human Leukocyte Antigen) from each parent. The statistics say that one in four siblings are a match. Well, Katie only had one, and one was all she really needed. We held on to hope that her sister would be that one. The doctor went over the entire procedure, risks, benefits, and all. But he didn't want to get too far ahead until we had the tests back. So we went back to waiting.

We spent a lot of our time during that visit laughing and giggling like we always did. I find that always stays the same no matter what we're going through as a family. The doctor also mentioned that one of the other positive things that would come out of this was that we would grow closer together as a family. I saw this happening from the beginning.

The medical field is not the only place where we like to have back-up plans. We have back-up plans in every aspect of our lives. Plan Bs and even Plan Cs, if needed. These plans make sense. Back-up plans are a good thing to have. Plans are good things to have. But I've come to realize, now more than ever, that our plans are really just that: *our* plans. We can plan as much as we want. Sometimes our plans work; sometimes they don't.

Plan A for Katie was that her sister would be a stem cell donor for her, a perfect match. Unfortunately, Kylie was not a match. Yes, we were disappointed. It was a slim shot to begin with, but not so slim our God couldn't work it out for us. I thought this could have been what we prayed and hoped for... that God would work out this perfect Plan A situation for us, that healing and answers to prayers would be tied up in that neat bow. That God would make it happen, even if the odds were against us.

We are taught to expect a miracle. To expect God to move. To expect good things for our lives. So I did. God could have healed Katie in an instant. God could have made Kylie a perfect donor match for her. God could have caused Katie's blood counts to go up miraculously. I expected that miracle to happen every time her counts got checked. Every. Time. It never happened, but I still expected God to move. I still expected healing—complete healing.

I didn't know how God planned on healing Katie. At this point, I knew it wasn't going to happen through our Plan A, which was the best way according to the medical professionals. But that was okay. I hadn't lost faith. Of course, I was disappointed, but I still knew God would get us through this journey. "One day at a time, Mama." That's all I kept telling myself. "One day at a time."

We moved on to Plan B, which I knew God could totally make our Plan A. He could use Plan A, B, C, D, E... whatever we wanted to label it. He could use it to our advantage and to His glory no matter what we called it.

The new plan became immunosuppressive therapy, our second choice, our Plan B. In a nutshell, the therapy included three different types of drugs Katie would receive in the hospital back home in Lafayette over the course of ten days. The drugs helped to accomplish one thing: killing the cells that were attacking her stem cells. We would be staying in ICU so she could be closely monitored for any reactions to these drugs, not to mention the fact that her immune system would be compromised through this, meaning her risk of infection was high. Over the next few weeks, Katie had to be seen by multiple doctors in preparation for this therapy.

The doctor informed us that every test came back negative for every single possible cause for aplastic anemia. Every. Test. Negative. There were no answers as to what could've caused her condition. None. But we still had to wait for the second biopsy results.

In the meantime, I tried to let Katie do as much as possible: having friends come over or allowing her to go a few places here and there, and even to church if she wore that darn mask. She didn't seem to mind it at all. One girl said to Katie, "Why are you wearing that mask? It's not like we have Ebola or something." I almost lost it —well, in my heart I did lose it—but then I kindly and sweetly explained what was going on to this ignorant girl. I hovered a little. I guarded her wherever she went. No hugs. No handshakes. Don't get too close. Katie most definitely didn't love that part. I was always around her. And, if I couldn't be, I had a reliable substitute.

Our lives were quickly changing from day to day. One minute I felt like we were doing great and had a handle on everything; the next minute we were falling apart and consumed by the unknown.

Katie began her immune therapy and did amazingly well during her second dose of meds. The only real side effect she experienced was that of skin reactions. Everything was running smoothly. The medicine was definitely working. Her white blood cell count plummeted to an extremely low 0.7, which was to be expected. To keep her as healthy as possible, our room was made into a reverse-isolation room, meaning the air was not being circulated in the room, but instead moved outside into the atmosphere. Everyone had to suit up to come in: masks, gloves, and gowns. We felt reassured that things were finally moving in the right direction. Treatment was going as planned.

Katie got lots of gifts and visits, as many as she could have in the ICU. There was an end in sight. This was just going to be about ten days. She was happy!

I remember so vividly her doctor coming in as she was halfway into her immune therapy. It was after 5:00 p.m. and I thought it strange for him to come by so late. Plus, we had already seen him that day. Richard had already left for the night and Katie and I had just finished dinner.

The doctor asked me where my husband was. I told him he had gone home. Then the doctor said, "Do you have a pen and paper to start taking notes?"

I didn't understand. I asked, "What's going on? There's so much information that I need to take notes?" He told me he was about to explain a lot of information to me. My heart sank. Wait... more information... *lengthy* information? Why? Haven't we already been through enough and learned so much about things we didn't even know existed? I really didn't want to know any more.

He had just received a fax from the lab with more results from Katie's last bone marrow biopsy. This time they did find more about what would be causing her aplastic anemia. There was an underlying condition.

He gave Katie a new diagnosis: myelodyplastic syndrome (MDS). MDS can cause aplastic anemia. MDS happens when the bone marrow cells do not develop into mature blood cells but instead stay within the bone marrow in an immature state. Like aplastic anemia, it is considered a bone marrow failure disease and also considered "pre-leukemia."

The treatment for MDS is a stem cell transplant.

There is no alternative treatment.

We were smack dab back at the beginning.

Because Katie was already in the middle of her immune therapy, the doctor decided to complete it. It wouldn't hurt, and perhaps might even help somewhat with her counts as we waited for this new treatment option to begin. The transplant process would now be expedited and potential unrelated donors would be searched for.

There were more tears after the doctor left the room. At one point, Katie said, "I just want this to be over. I just wanted this to work." I cried again. Richard drove back to the hospital to hear this news from me, then joined us in her hospital bed as we just held each other. The transplant doctor was right: we were growing closer as a family.

There would be many more moments of cuddling up together in hospital beds, but at the time, we tried to find the positive in this new obstacle. We talked about how this could be a blessing. MDS, if not treated, could lead to leukemia. MDS could be treated before that happened. We also talked about how it really didn't change much on the treatment options. We always knew a transplant could be the final option. We were staring straight at Plan C.

I looked at Katie and said, "God is still a Healer."

Through more tears, she replied, "I know."

EVERYTHING DOES *NOT* HAPPEN FOR A REASON
Daphne

God, who foresaw your tribulation, has specially armed
you to go through it, not without pain, but without stain.
- C.S. Lewis, *Letters of C.S. Lewis*

"Everything happens for a reason."

I can't tell you how many times people said this to us over these last few years. It started to get annoying. It actually made me question who God was. The God I had always known doesn't cause sickness or pain. The God I had always known doesn't kill kids, His kids, His own children. The very phrase, "Everything happens for a reason" sounded very much like, "God caused this so that you can learn something or become stronger," or, "God caused your daughter to suffer, be in pain, and face death for the betterment of other people." Excuse me, but my God does not work like that.

I began to stop people when they would say this to me. Someone would rub my back, and with a pity face and a quiet voice, utter, "Well, you know, everything happens for a reason." It was like hearing fingernails on a chalkboard. At that moment, walls went up, my jaw clenched, and I would reply, "I don't believe that."

I don't think "everything happens for a reason" is neither scriptural nor true. Sure, God has a plan. Yes,

He sees the future. Of course, the "steps of a righteous man are ordered by God." (Psalm 37:23)

But could it be that the hard things we go through are just that? *Hard things* caused by life? *Hard things* are directly related to one of the central truths of Christianity: the fall of man. We are not exempt from hard stuff and tough times. We should expect them. Why? Because we live in a fallen world.

Don't get me wrong, God knows when we are going to face tough things. I think He hates that for us. He weeps with us. He wants it better. He always has our good and the good of humanity in mind.

God does not need to cause or allow pain in His children to further His plan. And He doesn't punish us by making us sick. The world does that. Life does that. And, of course, the enemy would want nothing better than for believers to be dead. The enemy's whole purpose in life is to "steal, kill, and destroy." (John 10:10) That's his goal. It's plainly stated in Scripture. 1 Peter 5:8 says, "Your enemy, the devil, prowls around like a roaring lion looking for someone to devour." Not just *the* enemy, but, *my* enemy, and *your* enemy. He is our enemy. And he is proactively against you. He would like nothing better than to kill you, especially if your life is whole-heartedly devoted to God.

So why do we, as Christ-followers, still believe that God causes bad things to "happen for a reason"? We need to stop saying that and focus instead on taking the horrible circumstances that have fallen upon our lives and asking God how He can be glorified through them. How can God receive glory through our pain? Through our suffering? How we handle hard stuff is what matters. How will we face the hard stuff? Most of all, will we bring glory to God through it all?

I think people like to make sense of things by saying "everything happens for a reason." It helps them believe something good will come out of every bad situation. That's not always the case. A person doesn't always become better because they go through some trial. It definitely always changes them, but mostly makes them harder, more jaded, angrier, less trusting, depressed, hopeless. Of course, as Christ-followers, we would hope that this would not be how we would respond. We hope that we would run to God with all our might and desperately search for healing and restoration, whatever the circumstance.

When bad things happen, God simply wants us to cling to Him. He's not a god who sits up in the sky pointing a magic wand at us, deciding daily whom He will punish or hurt, deciding who He will reward or bless. His plans for us are *always* good. We don't have to doubt that. According to Romans 8:28, all things work together for the good of those who love Him. Because, despite tragedy, God can heal. God always heals. I still believe that. His answer to sickness is healing. His answer to death is life. God can use our story—or anyone's story —for His ultimate glory. I am thankful I don't serve a god who causes death and destruction; my God causes healing, life, and restoration.

I never had any doubt in my mind that God would heal Katie. She never doubted either. Sure, we struggled. Through our prayers of, "Lord, we trust you," we hurt. We cried. We got angry. But we always trusted God to do His work through our situation and be glorified. In one of my journal entries, I wrote, "Of course, God heals and will heal our Katie. There's no doubt about that. I don't know how or when, but He will."

I began to pray for God's best for Katie. What would God's best healing look like? I had no idea. In my mind, it would be her miraculously recovering from all she had gone through. That she was still alive after so many life-threatening situations was a miracle in itself. Learning to sit up on her own again after being bed-ridden for so long was a miracle. Pushing her frail little body to walk again just amazed me. My idea of healing was right in front of me: God doing the miraculous, here on earth, through the beaten-up body of my girl. Not only that, but God using all of this for His glory, through her testimony. She just knew that God was going to use this situation like that. She believed she would spend her life speaking to people, especially young people, about her story and inspiring others to live for Jesus. But that's not how God healed her.

There are many other phrases we use as Christians that I wish we'd stop using. Besides "Everything happens for a reason," there's "If it's God's will…" I can understand how someone who doesn't know God can say such a thing. But for the life of me, I can't understand why those who know God and have been devout Christ-followers for many years can utter these words.

I received message after message from well-meaning people with those words in it regarding my daughter's healing. "if it's God's will." Duh. *Of course* it's God's will to heal. God's will is *always* healing.

I would get angry when I heard those words. If you know God, then you know His will. If you don't know God, then everything is willy-nilly, up-in-the-air "theology."

When you say, "if it's God's will," what you're really saying is that you don't believe in the power of prayer. In fact, you don't believe God listens at all, much less intervenes in our lives.

Saying, "if it's God's will," means everything we're taught about prayer doesn't matter. It's like saying, "Well, you can pray as much as you want, but God's going to do whatever He wants to do, regardless." So then why pray? What a waste of time that would be.

The Bible always points us towards bringing our requests, prayers, and petitions to God (Matt. 7:7; James 4:2). In fact, the Bible says to pray about everything (Phil. 4:6-7).

Why would He ask us to do that if He were going to simply disregard them? What kind of god would command us to pray and ask, knowing all the while He wouldn't listen? That's not the God I know. The God I know doesn't just hear, but listens. The God I know sees and is moved by our honest pleas.

God's will is *always* for life and never for death. God's plans are *always* for good and never for evil. That's His will, so we never have to say, "... if it's God's will," as if we're giving Him an out in case things don't work out the way we think is right and good. He doesn't need our help, nor an out. We just have to understand that His ways are *always* higher than ours.

Jesus taught us to pray. In His prayer, He said, "Thy will be done on earth as it is in heaven." (Matt. 6:10) He could pray this with confidence, knowing who the Father is and that His will is perfect. As Christians, we need to take that phrase out of our speech. We need to commit ourselves to prayer, knowing full well He is working on our behalf.

We had put Katie's healing totally in God's hands. Whether God chose to heal her miraculously, which would, of course, have been our preference, or whether He chose another method was totally up to Him. Honestly, we had no other choice. We surrendered all control and said, "God, *however* You desire to heal our baby girl, we will accept it." We knew that God was the One who knew all, not us. At times, I would feel myself start to tense up, especially when I knew there was nothing I could do to control any part of this. It was out of my hands. I had done all a mother could do. I had to let go and trust God. I stopped praying for specific paths or ways for Him to heal her. To me, it was like saying, "God, here's the way we need You to work," like He needed me to lay it all out there for Him. I began to realize He has a history with healing and knows way more about what's going on than I do. He always knows what's best. So, I stopped telling Him how I needed Him to work. That can be a hard thing to do in dire situations. We see with our natural eyes what's obviously best. We know what makes sense in our minds. We know what will work for us.

But ultimately, we have to trust that God knows what's best. And, sometimes what may be best may not make sense to us at all. We may not see any good in our situation at all either. It may seem horrible to us. But, God always has a plan. His ways are always good. If we said we trusted Him, then our prayers would be, "God, You know what's best and we pray for Your best for Katie." That became our prayer. We prayed for God's best, no matter what that looked like through our eyes.

Every day, my prayers seemed to be the same. I lived out Matthew 7:7: "Ask and it will be given to you; seek and you will find; knock and the door will be opened to you." That's what I did. Day in and day out, I continued to seek, to ask, and to knock on that door. There was no stopping. I was determined to knock on that door to the point of annoyance. At some point, the door had to get opened for the knocking to stop. I know that if someone were knocking on my door for over a year, I wouldn't be able to stand the sound anymore.

I knew God was listening, but at the same time, He was silent. I knew He heard my cries, but I heard nothing from Him. Our circumstances, at times, seemed hopeless and just plain sad. The ups and downs were exhausting. There were days I didn't know what to think. I tried desperately not to let my mind take over too much and to keep taking all thoughts captive, like a good Christian should do. But sometimes that was impossible as I sat in an ICU hospital room all day and all night, listening to my child cry in pain and continue to suffer. I questioned where the "good" was in all of it because I sure didn't see it. I knew God could step in at any moment. But He didn't. So I waited, knocked, and hoped.

Richard and I would talk often about what we'd each been praying and about thoughts on our life situation and Katie's healing. In one of these conversations, I told him I wished there was some perfect formula to my prayers that would cause Katie to be healed and spring out of this place. I thought maybe I wasn't praying right… that I was doing it all wrong… that I obviously wasn't holy enough... that maybe if I were better at fasting... that maybe I didn't rebuke the enemy strongly enough... that maybe I just wasn't as close to God as I thought I was... that maybe, maybe, maybe.

As Christians, we are often taught to pray this way or that way. Make sure you do this or do that. Richard and I even had someone tell us we weren't praying with enough authority over her. We've heard all kinds of things you wouldn't believe. I began to realize that there wasn't some perfect formula for the prayers I needed to be praying. Katie's healing was not dependent on me or someone else or the way the prayers are constructed or spoken, as if it were some kind of magical spell. Katie's healing was dependent on one thing: God.

How dare we put so much weight on our prayers that actually elevate them above God Himself? A common misconception is the thought that God's healing is dependent upon this perfect prayer or the person who can pray this perfect prayer. He doesn't need our lengthy, flowery prayers nor our screaming, jumping-up-and-down prayers. He just wants honest prayers.

If Katie's healing hung on how good I was or how perfect my prayers were, she'd be in sad shape, unfortunately. If anyone's healing was dependent on us, we'd *all* be in sad shape. There was *nothing* more that I could do than what I was already doing. That was so hard for me to come to grips with. As a mom, I wanted just to fix it for her. Every day I had new ideas and questions to ask the doctors. Katie had to tell me herself to stop making suggestions. I just couldn't help it. Solving problems is what moms do best.

When I looked in the Bible, *every* time people went to Jesus for healing, He did only one thing: He healed. Every. Single. Time. He was *always* willing and never turned anyone away. There was no perfect formula. In fact, the only things I saw each person doing were: asking Jesus to heal and believing that He would. That's it. A lot of the people He healed weren't churchgoers either. Some were even those worthless Samaritans. Some were what most would consider unholy and not good enough. They didn't pray at all, much less fast. And what did Jesus do? He healed them. He told them their "faith" made them well. They believed He could heal.

I felt like we were in that same boat. We all believed, especially Katie, that Jesus heals and would heal her. Her faith remained strong until the very end. Any time we asked her whether or not she believed God was healing her, she would absolutely tell us, "Yes." She could have just gone through a life-threatening situation and been lying in a bed in the ICU and the answer would still be, "Yes."

Katie's hospital room, or should I say "rooms" (because there were many) were filled with Scriptures. We'd write them with markers on construction paper or color pictures from Scripture-based adult coloring books and hang them on the wall. We had her quote and declare them and they served as constant reminders of our faith. One Scripture that went with us from room to room was this one: *Rise and go; your faith has made you well.* (Luke 17:18) It reminded us that Jesus always healed.

There is *no* perfect prayer formula. There was nothing I could have done differently than follow the example of those healed by Jesus: simply ask and believe.

At this point, you may ask, "So why didn't Katie get healed? Why should we take prayer lessons from you?" The only answer I have is that she is healed. It's not exactly what we prayed for. We want her here with us. But is that what's best for Katie or what we see as best for us? Only God knew what was best for Katie.

I never thought we'd make t-shirts with our child's name on it because they were battling a horrible sickness. I put off doing it for the longest time. We weren't going to be one of those families with the t-shirts... the t-shirts people bought and wore as the child fought that illness... the t-shirts that faded in the wash and just became another t-shirt at the bottom of the dresser drawer... the t-shirts that people wondered whether they should even wear long after that family's child had died. We weren't doing that because Katie was different. She was going to be healed and this would be quick. There was no time for catchy name phrases and inspirational sayings.

The idea was brought up to us several times as a fundraiser. Finally, I succumbed to the pressure and we needed to come up with a design. Katie actually liked the idea of the shirt and decided she wanted to design it herself. One night, early on in this process, she drew out on a piece of journal paper how she wanted it to look, what type of shirt she wanted, and what Scripture would be hers. She chose Jeremiah 29:11, "'For I know the plans I have for you,' declares the Lord, 'plans to prosper you and not to harm you, plans to give you a hope and a future.'" This was the Scripture we constantly referenced in prayer and proclaimed as a family.

I've heard many sermons preached using this Scripture. We all have. The truth behind the Scripture lies in reading the whole book of Jeremiah, and not just the one verse. It is often misused when taken out of context.

The best explanation of this verse, in my opinion, was written in *Relevant* magazine in an article called "The Most Misused Verse in the Bible" by Chris Blumhofer*:

> We often read Jeremiah 29 like it is good news, plain and simple. But to the first people who heard those words, they were a tremendous disappointment. God's people had suffered terribly. They had lost their land, their throne, their temple. Before Jerusalem fell in battle, the people had given in to cannibalism. They were then force-marched

800 miles and paraded (literally) through a pagan city in which they were now considered as the living symbols of the power of that city's god.

It was into this kind of despair that Jeremiah offered God's promise: "I know the plans I have for you.... plans for your welfare and not for your harm, to give you a future and a hope." They were not easy words to hear. Jeremiah promised that God had a plan that was certain and inevitable. But it would not unfold on Israel's timetable. It would not simply undo Israel's hardship. Yet the promise stood: God would fully restore His people and bring them out of their desperate situation, but He would not do it in the way any of them would have planned it.

There's so much truth in that last section. When you're faced with horrible circumstances, it's hard to hear good news or even believe that good will come out of whatever the situation may be. But this is precisely when you need to keep reminding yourself who God is and what His promises are. If you don't, you will just fall into despair. I've been both places. I've felt such deep despair, but also such tremendous hope for the future. Through everything that had happened in our lives over the years, we, just like the Israelites, definitely would have preferred a quicker timetable, not to have experienced the hardships we had, nor the outcome. There are many things that parents should never have to see and experience. Those years were something I would never want anyone to have to face, to have to witness horrible things happen to their child. Yet despite what I think and how I feel about it all, it's what has happened, and the road we had to travel.

*Blumhofer, Chris, "The Most Misused Verse in the Bible," *Relevant* Magazine, Accessed March 22, 2017. *https://relevantmagazine.com/god/deeper-walk/features/21141-the-most-misused-verse-in-the-bible*

But just as God's promise stood for Israel, it stands for us. He fulfills His promise in His own way, in His own timing, and not always the way we want it. God's promise for us, as His children, is "a hope and a future." This Scripture *absolutely* refers to us, as Christ-followers, as co-heirs with Christ, and through Christ as descendants of Abraham. God never promised that life would always be easy and peachy-keen, but He did promise us "a hope and a future."

I've learned a lot about hope over the past few years. Hope is not a wish. It's not a desperate desire for something to happen. It's not even a dream for the future.

Hope is so much more than wishes, dreams, desires, and lofty goals… if your hope is in the right thing. If your hope is in something constant, reliable, and good, then hope becomes an assurance. That's what hope in God is. It's an assurance. Hope in anything else is just fairytale wishing.

Remember this old hymn?

> *Our hope is built on nothing less*
> *than Jesus' blood and righteousness*
> *I dare not trust the sweetest frame*
> *but wholly lean on Jesus' name*
>
> *On Christ the solid rock I stand*
> *all other ground is sinking sand*
> *All other ground is sinking sand*

But wait… the second verse is even better:

When darkness veils His lovely face
I rest on His unchanging grace
In every high and stormy gale
My anchor holds within the veil

On Christ the solid rock I stand
all other ground is sinking sand
All other ground is sinking sand

That second verse was my true life story. While Katie was in the hospital, I read a perfect visual of what hope in my unchanging God looks like. Holly Wagner (*Find Your Brave*) compared hope to floaties, the floats you wore on your arms as a child to help you stay above water. As a child, I trusted those floaties with my life. As a mother, I trusted those floaties with my children's lives. When those floaties were on your arms, you weren't going down. Not at all. They kept your head above water and they kept you from drowning. I trusted those floaties. I would not sink.

Hope in God looks like that floatie. I trust it. I put all my confidence in it. I know that He will not allow me to drown. He will keep my head above water. I can swim anywhere: shallow water, deep water, roaring water. Whatever the water is like, He will keep me afloat. That's not to say I won't get wet or get water up my nose or in my mouth; better yet, I might have to dodge a shark or two, and probably a multitude of jellyfish. There will be many, many times I have to remember to take breaths and remind myself I'm not going under. Most importantly, I cannot allow my floaties, my hope, to get punctured. Because if that happens, the air will leak out and I will drown.

And, if I'm being honest, sometimes that was the hardest part... keeping my floaties full of air. Keeping your floaties full of air is something only you can do.

eping your heart full of hope is your responsibility. u have to be the one who fills yourself up with all the hope that is found in God alone. You have to read God's Word every day. You have to remind yourself daily of who God is and who you are as His child. When you don't do these things, anyone can poke a hole in that hope floatie of yours. Or you can just allow the air to seep out by not carefully guarding that precious hope.

This Scripture is in the "Notes" section of my phone. I read it constantly:

"I will never forget this awful time, as I grieve over my loss. Yet I still dare to hope when I remember this: The faithful love of the Lord never ends! His mercies never cease. Great is his faithfulness; his mercies begin afresh each morning. I say to myself, 'The Lord is my inheritance; therefore, I will hope in him!' The Lord is good to those who depend on him to those who search for him. So it is good to wait quietly for salvation from the Lord." (Lamentations 3:20-26)

I'm learning and living this lesson of keeping hope alive. I have been stuck in moments of despair and hopelessness. And, I know that happened when I allowed myself to start sinking, when I forgot I had floaties on the whole time. I'm far from perfect and have had some real talk with God these last years. I can't say I won't have more moments of sinking and splashing frantically about in the water. Honestly, I can guarantee that these moments will come. But when they do, I won't drown, because I know my hope is in the One who will *never* allow that to happen.

Hope in Jesus is not a wish. It's an expectation. It's an "I know that I know, that I know, that I know He won't fail me" mindset. It's where "everything will be okay" comes from. It's a promise that can't be broken.

68

"It looks like we're stuck between a rock and a hard place." That became a phrase I used on a daily basis. One day, Katie looked at me and said, "Mama, that's my whole life." She was right. She began to say it every time we got bad news. She would look at me with that raised eyebrow and sassy expression and say, "Well, Mama... it looks like we're stuck between a rock and a hard place."

Each time we thought the rock may be moving, it would crush us once again. Our lives were ever-changing. Katie's health was up and down. During the last hospital stay, we were trapped again. Unable to move. At times, unable to breathe. Despite how hard we pushed, the rock barely moved.

Exhaustion would set in. We were tired. All of us. From pushing the rock. From having the hard place up against our back.

Richard would constantly remind me that we had no control over our lives nor over Katie's health. The only thing we could control was how we responded to what we were facing. Did we respond with faith? Did we respond with fear? Did we respond with doubt? Did we respond with complete surrender?

I have to be honest. I didn't always respond the right way. I was angry. I had been sad beyond belief, a brokenness I never thought I'd experience... total despair. I had definitely been scared.

Then my husband again became the voice of comfort when he would remind me that, no matter what happened, Katie would always be okay. He would say, over and over, "She wins! Katie wins!" He was right. She will always win. She wins because she has lived her life desiring only to serve God. She has lived her life loving God with all her heart. Many people have expressed how much she has been an inspiration to them in their faith, but she was an even greater inspiration to us as her parents. I don't even think "inspiration" is the right word. It's much deeper than that.

During that last week of her life, she was preparing to go to the operating room for yet another procedure. The doctors searched meticulously for what could be the cause of what was making her so sick. She expressed to me that she was scared to be put back under anesthesia once again, to be cut into once again. Understandably so. Katie's body had been through so much. We had worship music playing constantly in the ICU room that day and Bethel's song "No Longer Slaves" came on. She asked me to play that song on repeat. With labored breath, Katie began to sing the lyrics: "I'm no longer a slave to fear. I am a child of God." She was half-asleep/half-awake due to all the drugs in her system. I began to record her singing this over and over again. Little did I know that would be the last recording I would have of her.

She has won. She is no longer a slave to fear or anything in this world. She got her healing.

THE BIG DAY
Daphne

"I have heard your prayer and seen your tears. I will heal you."
- 2 Kings 20:5b (NLT)

We checked into the bone marrow transplant floor of Texas Children's Hospital on Sunday, August 2nd, 2015. We really had no idea what to expect for our stay. This was all so foreign to us. We just knew we would be there for at least thirty days.

The transplant floor was a small unit, only fifteen beds on one side of the floor, with a clinic for check-up visits and infusions on the other side. At the entrance of the unit, every person was met with a hand-washing station. Due to all these children's compromised immune systems, everyone who entered had to wash up. Each person was questioned when they walked in as to whether or not they had previously had a cold, cough, runny nose, fever, etc. The floor was meant to be kept secure and as germ-free as the staff could possibly make it.

We entered through the automatic doors and were greeted by two nurses, who showed us to our room: Room 39. It was the largest room on the unit, the "suite," we liked to call it. Little did we know how many times we would see this room again over the next two years. The nurse went over all the policies and procedures of the floor and gave us a tour. Only two people were ever allowed in the room at one time. There was also a family room with a microwave and a refrigerator where we could store our food. Two more rooms were for children: a play room filled with toys, books, puzzles, crafts, and board games, and a video game room. The families here got to know each other quite well due to the lengthy stay, and, sometimes, multiple stays.

We headed back to our room and met with our doctor, the head of the bone marrow transplant unit at TCH, whom we would grow to love and trust more than any other doctor. We weren't too sure about him at first. He was all about business and, with my crew, we needed some humor. But over the years to come, he and Katie became like two peas in a pod. She adored him and he became smitten with her. When Katie had an issue, she would tell the other doctors on service that they would need to contact him before doing anything she wasn't too sure about. Like Katie, he was no-nonsense, tell-it-like-it-is. They were exactly the same and communicated well because of that. She would tease him and he would chuckle at her comments and humor when he would visit every day. He just so happened to be the doctor on service that week, which made us more comfortable in starting this process. He went over the way this transplant would take place. I always asked a million questions and, most of the time, he had an answer for me.

Basically, the transplant would go like this: Katie would get five rounds of chemo. This chemo would be harsh during those days. The drugs would be ridding Katie of all her own unhealthy blood-forming cells with the intent of totally wiping them out. After that was complete, she would rest a day before getting her new stem cells, which would be from an unrelated donor, but a perfect match. A bone marrow transplant and stem cell transplant are the same thing, and the terms are often used interchangeably. The stem cells are taken either from the actual marrow (which isn't as common as it used to be) or simply from the donor's blood, like a transfusion.

These transplanted stem cells, once infused, would begin making their way to the actual bone marrow and start reproducing. The hope is that the new cells will produce healthy blood cells and immune cells, taking over the patient's entire system. If there are any remaining unhealthy cells, the hope is also that the new cells will see them as foreign and kill any cells that are lurking around. This is called "graft versus cancer effect." *That* is a good thing.

The main risk of a stem cell transplant is something called "graft versus host disease." This is where the donor cells see the "host," the patient's organs, as foreign and begin to attack one or more of them. This disease can be quite mild and dealt with through medication by suppressing the immune system, but there is a small percentage patients who get this severely. So severely that it results in death.

In a nutshell, that's how treatment works. If all goes as planned, the donor cells do their work. They multiply. We have a healthy child again, with no trace of any unhealthy or cancerous cells, and she can go on and live out the rest of her life like this was a bad dream.

Katie was first started on an anti-seizure medicine to prepare her body for her first round of chemo, which would start the following day. The most common side effect was, you guessed it, seizures. That's not easy for any parent to think about.

No one can really prepare you for what aggressive chemotherapy can do to a body. Worse yet, what it can do to your child's body. She needed me constantly. There was nausea, vomiting, headaches, chills, and overall fatigue like you couldn't imagine. But the harsher chemo was to come days later. After only an hour into this dose of chemo on that Friday, my baby girl started feeling the side effects intensely. Richard and I literally had to carry her to the bathroom. By the end of the evening, she had spiked a fever. Of course, they said the fever was typical and they treated it with heavy doses of antibiotics. She had a reaction to one of the antibiotics and broke out with a rash that they then had to treat with Benadryl. She was covered in petechiae (tiny busted blood vessels) from violent vomiting because her platelets were so low.

Long story short: chemo is rough.

At one point, Katie told me she just "didn't feel like [herself] at all." She had a hard time describing to me exactly how she felt besides just "not herself" or "not good." I had to wash her hair (she still had hair at that point) and bathe her. The first day was definitely the worst. She was extremely pale, almost a gray color, and she was lifeless. It was a very emotional day for Richard and me, seeing our daughter like that.

You can try to prepare yourself and read all about chemo. People can tell you about it, but you just never know it until you experience it. Everyone responds differently.

After the course of chemo drugs was complete, Katie got a rest day before her actual transplant occurred. We were thankful for it, because she felt a bit better after they gave her a new anti-nausea medicine, Marinol. This became a miracle drug for her throughout her treatment. It's THC-based so it was no wonder that, after her first few doses, she was attempting to make origami animals with her sister while eating three small bags of Spicy Sweet Chili Doritos. Yeah, it's that good.

As I look back on that day, I am thankful for the time we all got to spend together in Room 39. I am thankful Katie felt well that day.

Katie's stem cell transplant began at 1:32 a.m. on Thursday, August 13th, 2015. We anticipated and waited all day and into the night for that precious gift. We were quite tired when it finally arrived. The transplant itself was pretty anti-climactic, since it was a simple transfusion just like the ones Katie had been getting weekly. The difference is that this transfusion was to be the one that would save her life.

Richard, Kylie, and I surrounded Katie and prayed as her transplant began. It was very emotional for me, knowing what we'd been through and how long we'd waited to get to that point, but also knowing the hard stuff that lay ahead. It was an exhausting night. There was lots of activity: nurses in and out of the room, IV pumps beeping on and off throughout the night.

Katie insisted her sister stay the night that night. Seeing Kylie really perked up Katie more than we could have imagined. Kylie was always a bright spot for Katie through this. After a dose of Ativan for nausea, the sisters played Super Mario Galaxy for hours and had more great moments of laughter.

The side effects from the chemotherapy were still pretty bad. We rotated meds to help her with the vomiting and pain throughout the day and night. Unfortunately, the side effects linger for weeks afterward. Aside from the aforementioned Doritos, she hadn't eaten in a week. Actually, most teenagers who go through this won't eat for weeks, even continuing to eat very little after they are released from the hospital. They just don't have an appetite. This was normal. She was put on TPN (total peritoneal nutrition), which is an IV bag of nutrients she would normally get by eating, but this is administered through her veins. She would stay on that until she didn't need it anymore.

There were other side effects to come that don't show up until a few days to a week after transplant. Hair loss is one of them. Plus, not only was she in pain, but her vibrant personality was also gone. There were tiny moments when we saw Katie still in there somewhere, but seeing her like that was definitely difficult. Teenagers who go through this have a really tough time. So many feelings and emotions, combined with the pain… it's exhausting. This process requires lots of patience and perseverance. It's not a quick fix.

The waiting time began for the new cells to grow. The doctors explained it to us like this: a stem cell transplant is like planting a garden. The first thing you have to do is pull up all the weeds and till the soil and get it ready for new seeds. The new seeds are planted. Slowly, as the garden is cared for, the seeds start to grow and bloom. Over time, a beautiful new garden will appear.

This was my journal entry on Monday, August 17th, 2015, as we waited for those new cells to grow:

People ask me how I'm doing or what something like this feels like. The best way to explain it is that my life has stopped.

When horrible things happen in your life, it seems like time is literally standing still.

It's a place no one wants to be. It hurts. You feel trapped. It's hard to think about what's ahead. And, honestly you don't really care about what's ahead. Thinking that far in advance just becomes overwhelming, so you avoid it. At least I do.

As I sit writing this, I hear the drip of Morphine from my daughter's pump as she clicks that button over and over and over again. Knowing how much pain she's in is literally the most heart-breaking thing I have ever experienced.

Life stands still while everyone else moves on. Everyone else moves forward in their lives. And we are left behind in this spot, in this place, trapped in this moment.

It seems like everyone around you is moving at high speed, racing ahead of you and around you like a whirlwind. But you can't move. You're paralyzed. You want to scream, "WAIT! Hold up! Wait for me!" But you're just left behind.

I know that there is a way out. I know that it will come. But right now, it's hard to see.

People will comment and send me messages about how good it's going to be afterward. That is a constant. But I do wish that people would also realize that they don't have to say that. I know there will be relief at some point, that God will sustain us, that God will use this for good. But I'd almost rather people say, "I know this sucks! I hate this for you," than "Everything is gonna be okay."

I know that everything will be okay, but that doesn't make it not suck right now. Because it REALLY sucks right now.

Just because you're a Christ-follower doesn't mean everything in your life is gonna be flowers and rainbows.

In fact, it's quite the opposite. You're going to face some hard times. But you're also going to have some AMAZING times and live in God's blessings. I've experienced both. This, by far, being the hardest time.

I am trying to live out Scriptures like "be thankful in all circumstances," and "be content in all situations," and "when I am weak, He is strong," and "His plans for us are good."

I'm not going to lie. It's hard. It's hard to see your child suffer.

Two nights ago, Katie and I had a great little talk. This was the night before she experienced some of her worst pain. She's been pretty quiet throughout this whole thing, not much crying, not much talking at all. Richard and I had been concerned about how she was doing mentally and emotionally. She always said she was fine.

After we read our devotional, I asked Katie, yet again, how she was feeling. Not only that, but how she was feeling about what God was doing in this.

Finally, she had an answer for me and opened up.

She said that she thought God was doing two things: giving her a testimony to share and teaching her patience. She did admit to getting irritated. I think that's where the patience thing comes in. She's irritated that she can't sleep or eat. I would be too. She said she's "accepted this and she's over it." As in, "it is what it is, now let's get on with this healing."

I'm totally with her on this because God's doing the same things in me. Patience has never been my strong suit. And

I believe God is giving my whole family a testimony to share. He shows you so many things about yourself, your life, your family, your friends, and ultimately Himself when you go through hard times.

Because of this, our lives will never be the same. This has changed us. We will be different people after this. In fact, I think we already are.

That garden did finally grow. We were released from the hospital exactly thirty days from admittance. When I say "released," I mean we were released to an apartment in Houston. Patients have to stay in the area until at least one hundred days after their transplant in case any emergency should arise. Katie would also have to be seen in the clinic three days a week to check blood counts and how her body was responding to the transplant. We were discharged with lots of meds and knew we would continue to be in close quarters for a while. Katie would have to be away from people, and when we went back to the hospital, she wore a filtered mask to protect her from germs.

Katie's transplant seemed like a success. She was strong. She began to feel better. She was eating. And more than anything, she was anxious to go home. She missed her friends. She just wanted to be a normal teenager, to go back to school and to play sports again.

Katie only had one close friend visit her often, not only through transplant, but in the remaining years. It makes me sad when I think about it. Sure, she kept in contact with others through texting, but that died off the longer this entire process took. Still, I encouraged her to be thankful for her friend, Avery. Even at a young age, Avery knew what true friendship looked like. She and her mom visited us as often as they could. Katie so looked forward to those visits and would pray that she felt well when Avery was there. She loved her dear friend.

Finally, even before Day 100, on Thanksgiving week, Katie's doctor gave us the okay to go home. We packed up the apartment knowing we would still have to make this long drive once a week for Katie's clinic visit, but hoping that by the beginning of the following year, she would only need to be seen once a month and her care would be transferred back to her doctor at home.

The only glitch, it seemed, was that Katie was not one hundred percent donor in her blood. This was something that needed to happen. Otherwise, any rogue cell could start to multiply and take over, creating a risk of a relapse. At this point, what's done is something called a donor lymphocyte infusion (DLI). The donor would donate more cells, but this time Katie only needed t-cells (a lymphocyte—white blood cell—which would target any foreign/unhealthy cells and kill them off). She had two of these infusions before Christmas.

Katie really felt great while we were home. She completed schoolwork while she was homebound. I limited friend visits and made her wear her mask anywhere we went, which was still restricted. Things seemed to be getting closer to our new normal, and healing seemed to be in our grasp.

On New Year's Eve, I received an email from Katie's nurse practitioner that the infusions worked, and that, Katie was indeed now one hundred percent donor. Our little girl who lived one hundred percent with her spirit and soul was now one hundred percent in her body, as well. I cried such tears of joy. It was what we had prayed for. God had answered our prayers. It was our little Christmas miracle. I will always treasure those five weeks we were all together at home as a family.

THE RESPONSE
Daphne

"Share each other's burdens, and in this way obey the Law of Christ."
- Galatians 6:2 (NLT)

"Let me know if you need anything."

These were the words I heard the most through Katie's illness. Almost every day, or, as we got further along into the journey, every few days, people would send me messages that said just that: "Let me know if you need anything." Of course, after we moved to Houston, this all but came to a halt. The people we knew there were few and far between. Don't get me wrong; we had a couple of people who offered to help now and then, but it was nothing like the great response we got right after Katie's diagnosis while we were still in our hometown.

I get it. Time goes on and people go on with their lives. Add in the distance and we mostly got silence. The distance aided in the inconvenience of showing up for those in crisis. That seems harsh to write, but it's the truth. I know everything would've looked different had we been home. Well, I hope it would've.

Distance was definitely a huge barrier through these years. Typically, I gave people a pass. Surely, no one intentionally would abandon us. But as things progressed, I stopped inwardly enabling what I was perceiving as abandonment. Yes, I understand that people live busy lives two hundred miles away, but from our end, the silence was deafening. The next paragraph might feel really stern and blistering, but put yourself in our shoes, and read it with our context in mind.

We were in Houston approximately two years and there were family members and friends whom we considered family who *never* came to visit us. Not once to see us. Not once to see Katie. There were other friends who came to see us once. Once. In two years. One time. We felt like we were dying on the vine in the middle of nowhere, and we literally had no one due to that distance, or at least, that was always the reason given. But I'm done giving passes for the hurt this caused us because we were in Houston, not Helsinki. We were three hours away. That's all. We had made it a day trip multiple times. Yet it was too far for the people we had called friends for so long to travel just to come and see how we were doing, to pray with us, to hug us, to love on my sweet girl who was in so much pain. This is probably the harshest sting of all.

Don't get me wrong. I *did* have a few friends who did all they could to help me from a distance. Only a few. And when you go through crises, you will learn who's with you and who's not. You'll learn what true friendship looks like. My friend, Jeri, is the true picture of friendship. I've considered nominating her for sainthood. She's just really that good. She's the friend I wish I could be. She traveled to Houston, sometimes by herself, sometimes just for the day, just to sit with me, just to be a distraction for me, just to help me out. If she knew we had a need, she was there. I felt guilty that she would drive over as often as she did, but came to realize that's just who she is. The distance and drive didn't bother her a bit. Her heart was in this with me. She wasn't backing down, even when it got really hard. She had no answers or didn't know what to say, but she still showed up. She showed up more than anyone for us. I will never forget this and our friendship has deepened because of it. Friendships are formed and strengthened in the trenches. "Not all of us can be a Jeri," some of my friends said. But it should definitely be our goal and the friend we should strive to be. I want to be that kind of friend. I want to be a Jeri.

Right after Katie's diagnosis, people showed up in droves. It was extremely humbling. It was all new and fresh then. There were so many people saying they wanted to help. But when they would ask me what I needed or what they could do to help, I had no clue. People in crises don't know what they need. I couldn't have told you one thing I needed on a daily basis. The only thing I could think that I needed was that my daughter would be well. That was the only thing I "needed."

After I found out the news regarding Katie not having a transplant match within our family, I was disappointed. I cried. But Katie never wanted to see me cry. I brushed away the tears quickly and went on. I texted a few friends to let them know what was going on.

My friend, Sonia, simply texted back, "I'm on my way." That's it. I didn't ask her to come. I didn't want to put her out. I didn't want to be a bother. Most people in these types of situations feel this way. We just didn't want to bother or burden anyone with anything. Or even seem like we "needed" anything.

My friend didn't say, "Let me know if you need anything." She just basically told me what I needed. Because I didn't "need" anything really. Nothing. But she knew I needed a friend. She didn't have to bring me anything or even say anything. She was just there. That was huge. She picked me up, drove me around, and we talked. Nothing special. She asked me if I was hungry or wanted to just get something to drink. I could not even decide if I was hungry or what I wanted to drink. She offered all kinds of suggestions. I didn't know if I wanted even a bottle of water or a cup of coffee. I just didn't know. Normally, I'm a pretty decisive person and know exactly what I want or need. But that kind of decision-making stops when life hits you in the gut like this.

I made a blanket statement to everyone on my blog:

> *I say all this so that people know that I'm really not going to tell you what I need. I appreciate you saying you want to help and I appreciate the sentiment SO MUCH. But as each day goes on, I'm not going to call you or text you and tell you what I need. I hope that doesn't sound harsh. I simply don't have the mental capacity to stop and figure out who to contact when, nor what I need to begin with. So if you want to do something, just do it. That's the answer, right there.*

> *If you want to show compassion towards someone or you want to help someone in need, you just do it. Don't wait for them to tell you they need something. We kinda miss the boat when we do that, I think.*

> *If we're gong to be Jesus to the world, we shouldn't wait for a need to arise to put our faith into action. We should be proactive in our faith. Let's not wait around for someone to say, "I need," but be there in advance before the need occurs. Makes sense?*

> *Jesus didn't wait for others to come to Him and tell Him their needs. He went to them and told them what they needed.*

Seems like that's where we are now in our lives.

If God lays something on your heart to do for someone else, just do it. Don't wait for them to tell you to do it. Just do it.

In most cases, you probably already know what they need, anyway.

So instead of asking others how you can help them, just ask yourself, "How can I help?" God will give you the answer.

It's still so true today for me. Hurting people don't know what they need. Don't ask them. Just show up. Just do what God places on your heart. Don't wait around for them to let you know when they "need" something because that's never going to happen.

This was my journal entry on June 25, 2015, as we prepared to leave Lafayette for Houston for Katie's stem cell transplant:

"It's a marathon, not a sprint."

Someone made that very statement to me a while back. It stuck with me.

This whole journey on which we are embarking is a marathon, not a sprint.

People need to know that this is not a quick fix or process. Not only is the waiting long, but the recovery can also be long. I know people get anxious and then just get bored with the whole thing. They get tired of asking questions and again, like I've said in the past, people don't know

89

how to act around us. It's just gonna take time, guys. We'll get through it, but it's gonna take time.

Now don't get me wrong... I still remain hopeful. Katie is a very strong kid, always has been. She was strong-willed, and anyone who knows her has witnessed all this child is capable of, both good and bad. She has always been the picture of health. This child had no ear infections, no hospitalizations, no major viruses, no sicknesses at all... until now. I know she can beat any odds, especially with God on her side.

But as I've learned in recent weeks, recovery can take a while. We're talking months here. Actually, the medical field says a transplant patient isn't fully recovered and their immune system back to where it should be until after a year post-transplant. A YEAR!

Even more, there's more evidence for her and me to be away from home longer than expected. As another person told me... "no one goes home one hundred days post-transplant." No one.

That was hard to hear. Not just because I want my baby home, but I want us to be home with our family. I know that she could be the one... the one who has an amazing recovery and goes home early, but if she isn't, I need to be prepared for that, too. God will heal her either way, and that's all we desire.

There were tears from Katie just the other night as we got rid of our couch. She's emotional enough as it is right now, but she just wanted to lay on our couch (which we sold, because we're moving in just a couple of weeks... currently sitting around on patio furniture). She loves our house. She doesn't do well with change. Never has. And, her life is about to get flipped upside down more than it even has been the last few months.

I still cry. Not as much, but I cry.

When I think about being away from my husband and oldest daughter (who's about to leave the country), I get sad. I cry when I think about all that I will have to be for my daughter, thinking I may not be strong enough to do it. I realize I have to do it. I don't have a choice. But I wonder if I can be all that she needs me to be. I have to be strong. I have to be positive.

I get sad when I think of the possibility of us not being home for Thanksgiving, and let's not even think about Christmas. I can't bear that thought.

The thoughts that enter your mind when you're going through stuff like this span from the best, most positive thing to the worst-case scenario. I constantly have to take those darn thoughts captive... even crying my eyes out, I still take them captive and move on. You just can't allow your mind to stay in a hopeless spot. It wasn't meant to be there.

I have to keep expecting and hoping for the best, because that's what my God, my Father, would want me to do.

When I tell my girls I'm going to give them a gift, I would hope that they think that it's something good and not something harmful to them. When my girls think about me as a mom, I would hope they know that I would always want good things for them and their lives. And, of course, they know I want them well... I'm the one who takes care of them and always looks out for them, begging them to stay healthy.

91

It's the same with our God. He loves us even more than our parents, or we, as parents, can love our own children.

I know it will be a long time. I'm preparing mentally for that... crying all the same, but I'm preparing. I'm preparing for the marathon.

I see how people have been so loving and supportive and just plain old wonderful through this. But as time goes by, the calls and texts become less and less, the meals don't come anymore, the money stops, people just start to forget. Now I'm not blaming anyone. People have their own lives. I get it.

But, just know: running a marathon takes a lot of training. Weeks of training, sometimes months. There are those who are with you at the beginning... the sprint. In fact, there are SO many people who will be there for the sprint. But, thank God, there will be those who are with you through the long haul, through the whole marathon, all the way to the finish line. Those who will run right beside you, pushing you and saying, "You can do it".

Those people will be few and so extremely valuable.

Facebook posts can get you in all kinds of trouble. I try to edit each one in my mind beforehand, and question whether such a post would offend anyone. Sometimes I fail. I'm also convinced that someone will get offended at anything and everything these days.

This was a status update I posted as I was figuring out this whole "friends being there for us" thing:

"I am amazed at the compassion & love shown by people these days, but more amazed by the lack of it shown by some we called 'friends'."

I got texts and even a phone call from a well-meaning pastor saying I should take it down. I didn't. It was honest and I'm the last thing from fake. If some were offended, so be it. If you were one of the "friends" who dropped off the face of the earth, I don't particularly care if you were offended. If you were one of my true friends, you wouldn't be offended at all because you would have totally understood it. The thought for the Facebook post came out of something said by someone. I don't even remember what it was, but it definitely hit a nerve. The statement literally popped in my head and woke me up in the middle of the night. It had *nothing* to do with what people were "doing" or "not doing." It had nothing to do with "doing" at all.

People in our hometown were *fantastic* when the news of Katie's illness hit. They really were. That sounds like a contradiction, but go with me. When this was new, everyone was all in. Strangers in the grocery store would tell me they were praying for us. I was overwhelmed daily by the generosity, love, and support of people. My family and I are still extremely grateful for that initial outpouring. We have seen Jesus through so many people. And people may not even realize how God used them at just the right time.

I'm talking about community. Our community back home was so supportive. Our church family was amazing. I'm talking now about long-time friendships, or at least the friendships we used to have. After we became inconvenient and old news, some friends turned into acquaintances or just people we knew. It was heartbreaking. Their silence spoke volumes. That's the funny thing about silence: it only leaves inference, and it leaves the one doing the inferring to assume its implications.

I also left up that Facebook status because I am all about being transparent. I wasn't going to post only about how things were hunky-dory and fabulous as we went through this, because they definitely were not. That would make me a phony. I wanted people to see me... a real Christ-follower who loves Jesus with all her heart, just trying to live out her faith as much as best she could, as hard as it was, while being a regular mom/wife/woman (and friend herself), going through the hardest thing she'd ever faced.

That's the only way you can help others going through their own difficulties. Nobody wants to hear from somebody who has it all together. None of us *do* have it all together, but gosh, some people sure do look like it, don't they? How can we learn from each other if we're not allowed to show the deeper places in our hearts when we go through trials? I learn from reading about how other people got through hard circumstances. I *love* to know they had real feelings. It helps me to know I'm normal and not crazy or the worst person in the world for having the feelings I do.

So, back to the statement:

"I am amazed at the compassion & love shown by people these days, but more amazed by the lack of it shown by some we called 'friends'."

The word I wanted people to read was "compassion."

When situations arise in your life, a lot of times people, even friends, don't know how to respond or what to do. I get that. But it's important to realize during times like this, you *will* be disappointed by the lack of response or sensitivity of people you thought were your friends. Be prepared for that. I wasn't. This situation with our family changed some of our friendships. It's okay. But at the same time... disheartening.

I heard someone say this a long time ago and it stuck: "God gives us friends for a reason, a season, and a lifetime."

This is so true, and I have never seen it more evident in my life before now. I just have to learn to be okay with it because I am one of those life-timer friends. I go into every friendship like that and I expect everyone else to be like me, but that's not how life works. People are different. Hard stuff like this changes you. It also changes your relationships within your family and your relationships outside your family. Some are changes for the better. Actually, *all* are changes for the better, even if some relationships fall by the wayside.

As I reflected much on how friendship grows, changes, and fails through hardships like these, I came to a great realization about myself: I haven't been a good friend. If I expect others to act and respond in the way I think they should as friends, then I have failed miserably.

This was my journal entry on July 17th, 2015, the week before we left for Houston:

I know I pointed out I had some people who dumped me as a friend. But know that I have not been the friend that I expect everyone else to be.

Talking on the phone to one of my dearest friends a few days ago, I confessed to her that God had shown me that I should've been there more for her when she was going through a similar situation. I apologized for not doing more. I am embarrassed to say I did not even drive out to this friend's house one time. Sure, I called. Sure, I texted. But, that was not enough.

Sometimes when friends go through serious stuff, we think we should back off. We think we should give them time and space. We think maybe it's none of our business. We think they'll let us know when they want us to come around, when they need us. I'm here to tell you that, NO, they won't.

Now being smack dab in the middle of the same kind of thing as this friend, I KNOW I could've and should've done more. I should've texted or called more.

I was so consumed with my own life and used busy-ness as an excuse not to be a good friend. That's appalling.

Friendship takes sacrifice.

You know what that friend said after I apologized through tears? She said, "You were there." I think that was a pity "you were there" because I was not there nearly enough, y'all... not at all. What kind of person... what kind of friend doesn't drive out to someone's house to visit them during hard times?! A sucky friend. A friend who is going around with blinders on and who only sees her own life, her own stuff. A selfish friend. So, really not a friend at all. What's the point in having a friend if she's going to be absent when times get tough?

Not only am I learning to recognize what a good friend is, but I'm learning what it is to be one.

I'm committing to be a better friend, even more when times are hard than when they're not. Sure, it's easy to be there when things are easy... dinners, parties, trips, girls' nights, lunches, etc. Those are easy to be there for.

But friendship isn't always cute and pretty. Sometimes it's messy and not-so-cute. Sometimes it's hard. Sometimes we need to give more of ourselves even when we don't think we have anything to give. Sometimes the fear of not knowing what to do keeps us from doing anything. Let's face it: none of us want to be in a situation where we don't know what to say or do. It's awkward. It's uncomfortable.

I know now that I have not done enough in many friendships. I have not been there during hard times. I have been a fair-weather friend at times. But God is changing me to be the friend that I expect my friends to be.

I want to be there for my friends so much, but even more now than before.

You know what else that friend said to me after she lied through her teeth to pity-tell me I was there for her? She made this statement: "God allowed me to go through that so that I can be there for you."

Ding! {light-bulb moment} Geez. She's got so much more insight than I do into some of these spiritual things.

It's so true that we just don't know about stuff until we experience it ourselves. We don't understand what it feels like until we're in it. We don't understand how true compassion feels until we see it from the perspective of the one who needs it. And we don't know what it's like to be a good friend until we need one so much and have it shown to us by others.

Now that this good friend has gone through her experience, she's there for me in my own situation like no one else can be. Because she lived it.

My prayer is that I can do the same. My prayer is that I come out of this a better friend. My prayer is that I can be the one who is lifting up those who are going through similar circumstances.

To all of you to whom I haven't been a good friend, I'm sorry.

Let me interject a little here about the Church. Not *my* church, but *the* Church. Throughout all of this, I really came to love the Church. I saw the body of Christ be what it was created to be, and it seemed to be in direct contradiction to how my friendships were going.

Before this all happened, I don't think I really had a true love for the Church like I do now. Seeing the Church be the Church is a beautiful thing. There were so many people who came together and supported us through this time. And not just from our own church, but from other churches and denominations. Truly beautiful.

One Sunday, as Richard and I were on stage, singing and leading worship, a man came up for prayer. He approached one of the prayer team members and said, "I don't have a need. But, I came up because I wanted to stand in the gap for the Gaspard family and I want to pray for Katie." The prayer team member asked the man to pray and remarked at how powerful the prayer was. It astounded me that a man came down to the altar to lift up our family instead of his own need. Most people are there to pray for their own needs, which is what it's intended for. Not many go up to intercede for someone else's need. As I was singing these words, "I'm holding on to hope / holding on to grace / fully letting go / I'm surrendered to Your ways," someone petitioning God for me. What a perfect picture of the Church!

That's what it's all about: praying for others, standing in the gap for others, supporting others. We felt surrounded in prayer. We felt lifted up. We felt peace as

98

we walked through such a gut-wrenching time. I believe that's because the Church had us always before the Lord, praying constantly.

I may not have seen how beautiful the Church was before, because of all the negativity in some churches. But, when I looked beyond that, all I saw was beauty. I saw Jesus. I am forever grateful for the prayers of people over the years and the support extended to us by the Church.

As discussed in an earlier chapter, God doesn't allow horrible circumstances to happen to us because we need to "learn a lesson." I know this because He's a good Father and a good father doesn't create heartbreak and hurt for such a thing.

As a mother, I'm not going to slice off my child's finger and say, "Don't play with knives. Use them carefully. They're dangerous." Ridiculous, right? A good parent wouldn't do that. But good parents *will* guide their children through hard times... love them, hold them, help them in any way they can.

With that being said, God does speak through circumstances. When we listen carefully to His voice, we learn and we grow. And when tragedy comes, we listen harder, if that's possible. When we are faced with our own tragedy or hard thing, we become more compassionate toward others who are hurting. Our hearts ache harder. We understand in a deeper way.

I have learned more about what to say and how to react to others in their own tragedies and hard times.

So… how do you respond to a friend in crisis?

First off, *know this*: There is *nothing* you can say that will make it better. Absolutely nothing. While your sympathy and compassion are much appreciated, this is not a time for you to preach to someone. Not. At. All. Honestly, that has been the *most* annoying thing for me, for the following reasons:

Number One: I know God myself. You don't have to explain Him to me.

Number Two: I don't need you to tell me that God wants the best for me, or is working everything out for my good. I wish Christians would stop that. It's like our go-to when we don't know what to say. Please, just stop it.

Number Three: If you're going to send a Scripture to someone, make sure it's applicable and that God *really* wants you to send it.

It's almost like Christians don't want to face the facts and truth that other Christians can really hurt. And that bad stuff happens to them, too. It's like Christian denial.

I'm here to tell you: bad stuff does and will happen. Really bad stuff. Though you may be a Christian, you are not exempt. The only difference between Christians and those who aren't is that we have a hope when others don't. I can't imagine going through hard stuff without the hope I have through Jesus.

So Christians, don't try to tie things up in a neat bow and think saying, "All things work together for good," will make everything okay so you can wipe your hands clean of the matter. I promise you that's not what Christianity is about. Imagine if Jesus just walked around to all the sick, the dying, and the hurting and just gave them a hug, looked in their eyes, and said, "All things work together for the good," or some of those other Scriptures we like to quote. Thank God He didn't.

No, He looked at them. Saw their hurt. Felt their hurt. And then He healed them. Of course, I know He's

Jesus, the Son of God. But we should do the first three and leave the fourth to Him.

From this point on, I will not send the standard Scriptures people send to those who are facing hard times. Actually, I won't send any Scriptures unless I know, beyond a shadow of a doubt, God wants me to do that. Don't get me wrong... there are people who have sent me Scriptures that were just right, at the right time. But I received so many, I stopped reading them. I know... I sound like a horrible person. Really horrible.

A lot of times, as Christians, we can come off as "preachy" or "high and mighty" because we think we know best and we know everything. When someone is going through something hard, don't make it a time to try and think you understand or you can teach them something. You can't.

That's what I learned not to do. Here's what I learned *to* do.

Say what you truly feel. Don't be "churchy" and say what you think is expected. Sometimes there is nothing to say, and that's okay, too. But *do* say something. There are those, whom I thought were my friends, who said nothing. Not a word. Not a call. Not a text. Not a message. Nothing. So say something even if it's, "I love you," or, "I'm sorry," just say *something*.

Make that *something* simple. Sometimes, "I'm sorry for…" is all you can say. That's what you feel. Your heart breaks for them. You want to help them. If you really do, you say, "What can I do to help you?" Better yet, just do what you think they need. Life doesn't stop— people still need to be fed, homes need to be cleaned, laundry needs to be washed, oil needs to be changed. Find something practical and put your hands to it.

And lastly, pray for them. A lot of times we say we're going to pray, but do we really? I'm guilty and I'm sure you are. We get busy. We go on with our lives and it slips our mind. Commit to pray for that person, not only for them, but also for you, too. When you pray for them, God connects you with that person even more than before. In a nutshell:

Say something.
Pray something.
Do something.

I don't claim to be professionally trained in how to care for others. I am just a person who's been on the hard-times side a lot. However, I've been on the other side much more. Through my time on the hard-times side, God has taught me how to respond to others when they're on it.

He didn't cause Katie's illness to teach me that lesson, nor any other lesson, but I have learned nonetheless. He has shown me what it means to be the hands and feet of Jesus when others go through difficult circumstances. He teaches and guides when these circumstances occur when we lean into Him and listen.

I hope you will find a way to show up for those around you. Not just for those strangers to whom we can easily give and walk away, but also for your friends and family, especially when it gets hard and messy and it hurts.

THE EXTENDED STAY
Daphne

and that was the thing about her / she kept on
surviving / with bullet holes in her lungs / and knife
marks etched in her back / she never let anything get in
her way / resilient / a fighter / not by choice / but a
warrior at heart
- kiana azizian, *us: a collection of poetry*

Some time around New Year's Eve 2015, Katie began to not feel well. She first complained of a headache. Then came vomiting. After that, fever. For a few days, we were in and out of the ER in our hometown and on the phone with the doctors at TCH. It seemed like a virus, but her fever wasn't very high, so she was given antibiotics and anti-nausea meds. We were headed to TCH a few days later for her scheduled clinic visit anyway. But she wasn't getting better and her vomiting was accompanied by diarrhea.

The nurse practitioner had us come in early and told us to "pack an overnight bag just in case." I remember the drive to Houston that day. I gave Katie a strong dose of anti-nausea meds, hoping she could make it the whole way without getting sick. She slept most of the ride.

We arrived at the clinic. Katie was seen and, just as the nurse practitioner anticipated, was admitted so they could run more tests. By this time, she was quite lethargic and the nausea/vomiting/diarrhea continued to get worse.

That overnight stay started January 5th, 2016 and didn't end until November 11th, 2016. Katie was so sick during those first couple of weeks inpatient. The doctors ran test after test, trying to determine what was causing all of this. Every test for viruses, bacteria, fungus, and the like came back negative. After a week, we got the final, dreaded diagnosis: graft versus host disease.

This was my journal entry, January 13th, 2016:

As I write this, I'm sitting in a place I never thought I would write in again: the hospital room in the bone marrow transplant unit at Texas Children's Hospital. We're here again. We've been here a little over a week.

We've had some extremely scary moments, moments I wouldn't wish on any parent. I've cried my eyes out. Richard's cried his eyes out. And, last night, Katie cried her eyes out.

While we know that God is with us, it's still a hard place to be again.

Two nights ago, we didn't really know that our girl was going to make it. It was the scariest thing I've ever faced. I listened to her moan in pain, in her sleep, as she was on pain medicine. And all I could think of is that she was making the same sounds my grandmother made as I sat with her in the hospital when she was dying of cancer. It was horrible, knowing that not much could be done about the pain.

What was even scarier was being here so long with the doctors not knowing what was going on so they could treat it properly. There was lots of waiting and no answers while our child was suffering.

The blow that we didn't expect was the diagnosis that she was given. I had only been expecting good things. The doctors said she has GVHD (graft versus host disease)... severe GVHD in her gut. It took them longer to figure it out because her symptoms were unique and she didn't present the standard symptoms associated with GVHD. The GVHD was not just in her gut, but is more systemic and has affected other areas, including her respiratory system, which was why she was also having breathing problems.

With that being said, we will be in Houston for a while longer. Apparently, GVHD of the gut is the most difficult to treat.

We always knew this was a risk, but never thought it would happen because we, again, always expect the best. They did tell us this may happen, but it is rare. The doctors here are no strangers to this disease.

So we find ourselves in the same place for a while longer. Let me tell you... it sucks. There's no other word for it.

I honestly never thought she would be the one to get this. Of course, I never thought she'd have to have a stem cell transplant, either. She had been so healthy, yet again, even after transplant. But these donor cells were attacking not only her GI tract, but also her lungs and her liver at the same time. Katie was immediately started on high-dose steroids to suppress this new immune system attacking her body. Within hours, her lungs cleared. She perked up. She wanted to take a shower and watch a movie. Yes, this was working! Or so I thought. But we would have to wait and see how this all played out: how long treatment would be, the dosing of the steroids, the length of the hospital stay, and those sorts of things.

The only problem: Katie's GI tract did not clear so easily. She was still nauseous 24/7 and was still vomiting, but the diarrhea had gotten more extreme. She, of course, wasn't able to eat or drink, so they put her back on TPN for nutrition, which made her extremely sad. It seemed like the light at the end of this tunnel had become farther out of reach.

A few days after the general GVHD diagnosis, we got the news that Katie had the most severe kind of GVHD: Stage 4 GVHD of the gut. It was one of the worst cases they had seen at Texas Children's Hospital. You can imagine how upset Katie was when the doctors told her it would be a while until she would be able to have anything to eat or drink. She was only able to suck on a few ice chips now and then. Her gut needed rest. It was inflamed, and any little thing could irritate it, and there was also a risk of perforation or tear in her intestines and colon.

Not only was it agonizing to watch my child in constant pain, but add constant hunger and thirst to the mix and I felt helpless. She was put on a whole slew of immunosuppressive drugs in addition to the steroids, antibiotics, and a Morphine pump for pain. Her pumps worked overtime, day and night. Something was always being infused. One doctor gave us this illustration: imagine you have a bad abrasion or wound on your arm and how long that takes to finally heal. It was the same thing in Katie's gut, but it was on every inch of her GI tract. All the pieces needed to rest and heal.

We knew this was going to take some time. Months at least. We were stuck in this waiting game yet again. We all cried a lot. This was heartbreaking. Seeing Katie in pain was definitely always the hardest part.

January and February passed by painfully for Katie as we continued to wait for her gut to heal. If the severe GVHD wasn't bad enough in itself, she had contracted viruses due to her weakened immune system. Such viruses wouldn't even affect you or me, but they could actually kill my girl. One virus, the BK virus, debilitated her. This typically wimpy virus lives in most of us but caused severe spasms and bleeding in Katie's bladder.

This went on for three months. She would moan in pain most days and find the most comfortable position, which was on the toilet, where she sat one day for twelve hours despite everyone urging her to get up. She was miserable. The doctors dosed her pain meds high, but told us there wasn't a whole lot that alleviated this type of pain. The nurses would encourage Richard and me to take breaks, as the sound of her being in pain twenty-four hours a day was too much for us, too much for any parent. We would swap out from time to time and go to the family room just to try to keep our minds clear.

Fast forward to March 2nd, 2016. This was my journal entry describing Katie's next hurdle:

"Critical" was the condition Katie was in last week as we found ourselves in the PICU for three days.

Early Tuesday morning, Katie woke up vomiting. She had been vomiting for a few days, but it seemed different from before. She was having more nausea. The vomiting that occurred that morning and that would continue over the next day became more bloody and in high volumes. It's sad that I now can differentiate between fresh-blood vomit and old-blood vomit. But it's something I've had to learn, along with so many other countless things I never wanted to even know about.

That morning, as I was helping Katie back from the bathroom to the bed, she collapsed on the floor. Most of the nursing staff rushed in to help get her to the bed. She was unable to put any weight on her feet or use her legs at all.

As she fell to the ground, she said, "I just have to lay here for a little while." There was no getting her up without help. As the nursing staff was helping, she became incoherent. One nurse was calling her name over and over and saying, "Katie, are you still with us?" No answer.

This was, by far, the scariest moment yet, until another one that would soon follow.

The nurses eventually got her back in bed after about thirty minutes of trying. Turns out she had lost a large amount of blood. Her hemoglobin was the lowest it had ever been... dangerously low. Her platelets were equally low. The string of transfusions began.

The GI doctors and surgeons were called to consult and she was scheduled for another scope the next day. The vomiting and blood loss continued throughout the night and she ended up getting the procedure done earlier in the morning. Our doctor was extremely anxious to get her down to the operating room.

Richard and I sat in the waiting room. We waited. And waited.

Some of my very best friends had actually driven up for the day; unbeknownst to them that this was a day I was really going to need them. They sat with us.

Over two hours later, the doctor came out and took us into a private room. During this time, he proceeded to tell us that at the base of Katie's stomach, near her small intestines, she was oozing blood. There was no certain vessel or anything that could be cauterized or taken care of. No quick fix. She basically had a large bleeding ulcer at the top of her small intestines.

The doctor said she was in critical condition and that she would need to be monitored in the PICU. They had to give her twelve units of platelets and four units of blood just in the two hours she was in the operating room. They called even more doctors into the operating room to consult as she was on the table. She needed to get stabilized and they needed to try to stop the bleeding with medications. Overnight they would monitor her and be able to give her blood more quickly if she needed it. They also had placed an NG tube in her stomach to suction out all the blood so that they could measure how much was coming out. If the volume of blood was large and they couldn't get her bleeding under control, they would have to go in the next day to scope her lower than they were able to. Depending on what they saw then would determine if, as the doctor said, they would need to "open her up."

I'm sorry. What? "Open her up?"

This is not something you want to here as a possibility for your child who can't seem to stop bleeding.

The next twenty-four hours would tell us which way this would go.

I have figured out on this roller coaster ride that being scared is a very real thing.

And that being scared happens even when you trust God. It's part of being human. I don't beat myself up over that stuff anymore. There are moments when I'm definitely scared. And, there are moments when I definitely rest in God's arms.

Our time in the PICU was LONG. It was emotional. It was certainly uncomfortable as there are no couches in the rooms. Sleep was limited during this time. We were all exhausted. We lost our room on the BMT floor and had to move all our things out. Thank God for our friends who were here exactly when we needed them. They prayed with us, held our hands, hugged us, and moved all our stuff. Coincidence they were here on this day? I think not.

After the second night in the PICU, seeing countless containers of blood being pumped out of Katie's stomach, something immediately changed. I know that it was God moving on our girl's behalf and in her body. Within just a short couple of hours, the container of blood was no more and the only thing coming out was normal stomach stuff... bile and normal water/secretions. They continued to monitor it.

Katie hated not being able to shower or bathe. Like a good daddy, Richard washed and conditioned her hair using a basin. It helped her feel so much better.

By late that afternoon, a room became available back on the BMT floor and we were outta there. I'd never thought I'd see the day Katie was crying to go back to the 8th floor. It's what she knows. It's where she's comfortable.

Everyone knows her there. She even gave the doctors a hug and cried about being able to finally go back up.

This was our second "serious" or "critical" moment. We had an earlier one before this, involving her kidneys, and the words "kidney failure" and "renal failure" were also used.

This is a very bumpy road that we're on. Just when she's improving in one area, she seems to experience setbacks in others. But no more. I've had enough of this. This particular setback was caused by the treatment (steroids) for the GVHD.

There are so many other things going on that just would be too much information to post, but just know that this thing she's fighting is a beast. Not only physically, but mentally and spiritually. As I've told her from the time she was a little girl: the enemy would fight against her. He would like nothing better than to see her dead. He ALWAYS comes to STEAL, KILL, and DESTROY. Katie has always been a force to be reckoned with and we've known from the beginning that she had a great call on her life. It's never been more evident than now.

I hold this Scripture close:
He will cover You with his feathers and under His wings you will find refuge. Psalm 91:4

I find myself hiding most of the time...

Hiding.

Simply hiding under His wings.

113

Although I don't understand most things about what we're going through, I still know He hides me. He holds me. It s the only place we can feel safe when life is hard and we have no answers. Even when we don't know where He's leading us or what He's doing, He still hides us. We can still hold on to Him for dear life. With everything that's within me, that's where I am. Not knowing. Not thinking. Just holding. Just hiding.

As time went on, Katie experienced multiple GI bleeds with lots of blood loss and trips to the PICU. After another three months practically living at Texas Children's Hospital, I became accustomed to it. I'd even say I became quite comfortable there. It had become routine.

It's a sad day when hospital life and the near-death instances with your child become the norm.

Katie also became comfortable with it and considered it her home. She began to not care when she would ever get out. Her only concern was being pain-free.

"Home" became the hospital. I grew comfortable with the pullout couch... with the daily routine... with the Keurig machine in the family room... with the very heavy IV pole I had to get over the threshold to the bathroom... with the full parking garages... with changing a hospital bed... with the ice machine adjacent to our room... with the wait for a washer on the 16th floor... with the view of MD Anderson from our window... and, most of all, with the nurses and doctors. They actually became our family.

At the end of March, the doctors started talking about discharge. Yes, discharge. They didn't say it was going to happen, but simply that we could start talking about it. That day, Katie collapsed again, unconscious, but this time on the bed. She was unresponsive to me,

114

which sent me out the door, yelling, "Help! Help in here!" Before I knew it, there was a team of people in the room. She was given oxygen and an immediate battery of tests. Once she regained consciousness, she realized what had happened—again—and started to panic. This was scary for both of us.

Her fainting, it turns out, was due to the same reason as before: losing blood. She had been vomiting earlier in the week with more blood, and her hemoglobin had dropped drastically again. The doctors pumped her full of blood, platelets, and plasma, then drew blood for all kinds of tests and did an ultrasound. She was even sent down for an MRI.

After everything came back, it seemed she had a bacteria in her blood—the same bacteria that was most likely the cause for the step backward with her GI issues that had been occurring the previous days.

I wrote this in my journal after that day:

Your faith does not make things hurt less.

Your faith gives you comfort through the hurt and hope for the future.

When you walk through hard stuff, it just hurts. It hurts terribly. There's no way around it.

I learned to LEAN IN to the hurt and not bury it or try to distract myself from it. God is in the hurt. There's healing when you lean in. God wants to hear from us in the hurt.

We may not get the answers we want, but He still wants us to tell Him our fears and concerns. He comforts. He holds us. And when we truly love Him, we have to truly trust in His plan, even when we don't understand it.

Today, and every day, that is what we do. We simply have to trust. We have to trust in a God to whom we dedicated Katie, as a baby, long ago... that He would protect her... that He would guide her... that He would watch over her... that He would use her to further His kingdom. We just have to trust, comfortable in knowing He's got this under control.

Needless to say, there was no talk of discharge for a while after that. Katie was, of course, discouraged. We were too.

This was my journal entry, April 13th, 2016:

"Fight or die?" That's the choice I tell Katie she has when she wakes up in the mornings saying she can't do this for another day. I ask her what the alternative is. There are only two choices right now: fight or die. If you're not going to fight, if you're going to give up, then the choice is death. If you say you're going to fight, it's going to be hard, REALLY hard, unbearable at times, but you have to push through.

I say this to myself every day when I wake up with tears streaming down my face, knowing I also have to face another day of this... a day of watching my child hurting, a day of no answers, a day of not knowing what the future holds, a day of waiting, a day of heartbreak over what has been stolen from my sweet girl and our family. I cry. I wipe the tears away. I ask God for help. And I get up again.

Is it hard? Absolutely.

But I have no other choice. I have to fight for my daughter as she fights for her own life.

I am weepy as I type this because it is exactly a year ago today that I rushed Katie to the ER after lab work ordered by her doctor.

My girl's different, not just physically, but mentally. I scarcely can remember my fun-loving girl. Chronic pain and near-death experiences definitely change a person.

When I've asked Katie, after she says she's scared, about what she's scared of... fighting or dying, whatever it may be, she says she's not afraid of where she's going, just afraid of being without us. Oh my heart. And this is why she fights. She said she would live every day in pain if it meant she could be with us. Oh my heart again... aching, breaking.

There have been many ups and downs, many tears shed. Just when I think I have no more tears to shed, they come again.

I have had a broken heart before... many times. But never like this. I feel my heart break a little more each and every day. I think it's not even a heart anymore, but just crumbled pieces of what it used to be. Unrecognizable.

I am unrecognizable to myself. We are all unrecognizable at this point. I have lost my passion for anything. I have no desires, no wants. I feel dead inside. My only desire, the only yearning of my heart, is healing and health for my girl.

There are honestly days where I do feel hopeless, despite the fact that I know God is very present with me. Despair has become my closest friend. It's a very dark place to be.

117

*Waiting for God to move, to answer, to provide the
?, to heal.*

*ı m sure you are appalled that such a "strong" Christian
could be in such a place. But I'm here to tell you that it
happens. And it happened to so many in the Bible who
were close to God.*

*David wrote this and it so adequately expresses my inner
self at this moment:*

*Day and night, I have only tears for food, while my
enemies continually taunt me, saying, "Where is this God
of yours?" My heart is breaking as I remember how it
used to be. I walked among the crowd of worshipers,
leading a great procession to the house of God, singing for
joy and giving thanks--it was the sound of a great
celebration! Why am I discouraged? Why so sad? I will
put my hope in God! I will praise Him again--my Savior
and my God!
--Psalm 42:3-6*

I weep.

*The enemy taunts me, asking "Where is God, your
Healer? Why would He allow this? Why would He not
rescue your daughter from such pain? Where is He?"*

*My heart breaks a little more each day and I'm reminded
of our life before this.*

*I'm reminded of the years my family has served in
ministry.*

*Our life has become something we don't recognize nor
understand.*

118

I'm reminded of all the truths I've learned throughout the years of serving God.

Yes, I am discouraged and sad...

BUT STILL, I put my hope in God and praise Him for who He is.

No matter what, we will praise Him. No matter what, we will serve Him.

That's not to say we don't and won't hurt, but STILL we cling to Him.

It's the only thing we know to do. We know He is faithful.

Katie would spend the next few months in and out of PICU. She actually spent just as much time there as she did on the bone marrow transplant floor throughout her years at Texas Children's Hospital. As one of the PICU doctors said, "On paper, Katie looks like a lost cause. But then when you come in and see her and talk to her, you think she's gonna make it and all these things are manageable."

She had more than her share of hurdles to get over. The GI bleeding became frequent. We would watch as the PICU team would push large tubes of blood into her veins because she was losing blood too quickly. We would watch her blood pressure tank until she became unresponsive. We would watch her start to need oxygen. We would watch our sweet girl pass so much blood that she would be laying in a pool of it from her shoulders to her feet. This was so hard. It was something we saw on many occasions.

The doctors performed multiple upper and lower GI scopes on her over those months and years. In April 2016, she went for another emergency scope and came back to the PICU room intubated. This was the start of a long, two-month stint there. Katie became bedridden; her kidneys had completely shut down due to the multiple GI bleeds and some of the medications. She was placed on CRRT (Continuous Renal Replacement Therapy), which means she was hooked up to a dialysis machine twenty-four hours a day, unable to move. Because of this, her already weakened muscles began to atrophy more and she lost her ability simply to sit up on her own. Meanwhile, the steroids had caused issues with the rest of her body: bone loss, fractures in her spine, skin thinning and tears, and, of course, the biggest issue of an ulcer just at the base of her stomach.

The bit of good news we had received during this long stay was that her GVHD, the main thing that had gotten us to this point to begin with, was under control. This meant that the steroids could slowly start to be weaned and healing in all the other areas could begin. The road ahead was still long and painful.

I wrote this entry on June 10, 2016. It is the perfect picture of what life was like those long days in the PICU:

Exhausted … That's literally all I feel.

But our lives have become exhaustingly repetitious. It's the same thing every day, without much change at all. It was that way on the BMT floor for months, but it's definitely worse now in PICU.

My day starts and ends the same way most every day.

I wake up and throw on some sort of workout pants, t-shirt, and tennis shoes. I pull my hair back into a ponytail and put on only enough make-up to make me look alive. I pack up my backpack and anything Katie might want from the apartment and head over to the hospital. (Because she's in PICU, the only option available for sleeping parents is recliners in the waiting room. We used them the first two times we were in PICU and knew that the use of them for an extended stay was just not gonna work. Talk about exhaustion! Every night we return to the apartment to sleep.)

Richard heads off to work most every morning, but is able to sit with Katie some mornings/days. This is a huge break for me.

I make the short drive to the parking garage and then make the trek to the hospital… third floor, PICU. I check in and get my daily "I don't have flu symptoms" sticker and my badge that allows me back in the room. Only two visitors are allowed in the room at a time and must have the badge. At this point, I walk in and the receptionists don't have to ask what bed number badge I need. They know me.

I pass through the waiting room. I pass by snoring dads and grandpas. I pass by moms weeping. I pass by chatter filled with medical terminology. I pass by friends and family holding each other, consoling each other. I pass by new parents getting the speech on how the PICU works.

I get to the hand washing station and wash up, then press the intercom button to have the door unlocked.

I head to Katie's "room", or should I say "bed"… Bed 29. Today marks five weeks she's been in this bed.

I talk to her nurse, ask about the evening, go in and let her know I'm there.

This is the start of her day. She's just starting to wake up.

She gets physical therapy late morning. Before that, there's all kinds of other things that have to happen: she has to get off dialysis (They take her off for an hour each day because her physical therapy needs are so great.), she has to take her oral meds, try to eat a little something, and MOST importantly get her pain and anti-nausea meds before physical therapy starts. Some mornings, I have to familiarize a new nurse with the plan so that they are up to speed on everything. It's SO easy when we have the same nurse multiple days in a row. That does happen, but not enough, in my opinion.

Physical therapy is a chore for Katie. She's in pain and she's going to be in pain until she is stronger. I'm not sure if I've been clear about how weak our once-super-strong girl actually is. Katie is unable to hold herself up due to weeks of being in the bed and the steroids weakening everything. She can sit up in the bed with the support of the bed, but cannot hold herself up. Therapy for the last couple of weeks was just getting her to sit at the side of the bed with her feet hanging off the bed. She has a compression fracture in her spine, which has made her pain pretty bad at times, mostly during physical therapy. She has been able to move to the side of the bed with help and support, then hold it for short amounts of time. She does exercises lying down in the bed also to try to strengthen her legs and arms. She's also been having some neuropathy in her feet and toes. That's another thing she gets pain meds for.

The last couple of days, the goal has been to get her from a lying position in the bed to a reclining wheelchair. The therapists physically move her from the bed into a chair that is actually flat like a bed. Then they slowly begin to elevate her head and back while lowering her feet and legs into a chair position. This whole process is difficult and painful for her. It's extremely hard to watch and to hear her moan or scream in pain. Some days I have to leave the room, despite her cries, because I just can't handle watching her in pain. The therapists always encourage me to leave and express how hard this is on parents. But Katie always wants me to stay. There are days when she says she can't do it, but we make her do it anyway. Each day she doesn't do therapy or sit up is a day she gets weaker. Each day she does do it, she gets stronger.

Today, she was actually able to pass and kick a beach ball while in the chair. This was huge. Every day, they try to push her a little bit more. Even if everything else was going great with her condition right now, we wouldn't be able to leave because of how weak she is. She HAS to be able to sit up and be stronger to leave.

When she gets back to the room, the transfer back to the bed is just as hard as the transfer to the chair. Once she's settled, I try to get her to eat something.

You see, her GVHD has improved. That's something to be thankful for. She's actually been able to eat a little bit. The only problem is she says that nothing has a taste. EVERY SINGLE THING we try of the foods she can eat... no taste. It's frustrating for her and for us. Eating is something that should be enjoyed and give her some comfort and she's not able to have that. We want her to eat to see how her stomach will absorb nutrients and then her IV nutrition could be reduced. The doctors say she will probably be on IV nutrition for a while until they know for sure she's absorbing what she's eating. They are starting one of her IV meds orally today and then will check her levels on it. That could be the sign to show us if she is or is not absorbing.

The rest of the day includes waiting for doctors and trying to make Katie comfortable and distracted. The days are long. I sit in the corner of the room in the most uncomfortable plastic chair. Richard calls it the "medieval torture device." I look out the window as the sunlight comes in and see only more hospital building around me.

The nurses are great and one particularly amazing nurse rearranged Katie's whole room to give her a different view. Now, she can see out the window. When her BFF Avery came to visit yesterday, the nurse had bought decorations for them to use to brighten up her room.

That was a great day. I thought seeing her friend would make her super emotional. She had cried the day before the visit, saying, she "always wanted to be a role model for her" and "like a big sister because she didn't have that like [she] did" with Kylie. I promised to bring her friend over for a very long visit when Katie makes it outta here.

She misses her friends and her people back in Louisiana so much. Visits are a bright spot in her long, dreary PICU days.

I don't think I realized how much Katie has changed until I saw my friend's reaction when she saw her yesterday. To me, she looks like she has been looking the last few months, but I see her every day. After months of not seeing her, it was emotional for my friend, who has always been close to my sweet girl too. I don't think Katie thinks she looks much different. She knows she's changed, especially thanks to steroids. Her puffy face is the most significant change that people see.

As she rode in the wheelchair on the busy third floor yesterday, out in public for the world to see, there were pity stares. It didn't bother me at first. We got that when she lost her hair or had to wear her mask. It wasn't a big deal. But at one point, I just wanted to scream, "This is not who she is." When people look at her, all they see is a very sick kid. They wonder what's wrong with her, what's her story. They feel pity. I don't blame them. But I want to tell them, "She's SO much more than this!" I could give you a list of things that describe her, but "sick" is not one of them. Just writing about this makes my eyes swell up with tears, so let's move on.

Sometimes Katie is up to watching a movie, sometimes nothing. Some days she just wants to nap. Last week, she gave herself a manicure. But, every day I encourage her to do something. Sometimes I succeed; sometimes I don't.

By evening time, Richard arrives at the hospital from work. We talk, try to spend more time with our girl if she's up to it. Shift change happens. We make sure Katie is good and tucked in... make sure she's got her phone, her bunny, her eye mask, and any other things she might need overnight. We tell her, once again, how AMAZING she is and how GREAT she's doing. We read her devotional and pray before she goes to sleep.

We make the trek back to our parking garages and head back to our apartment. At that time, I know I have a good hour or two to eat, bathe, maybe do some laundry, clean up a bit, and watch some TV. I just want to escape this day.

Then I go to bed and do the same thing the next day. I go to bed exhausted. I wake up exhausted.

Yesterday, a meeting was held between Katie's BMT docs, renal docs, PICU docs, and physical therapists to create a consistent plan for her care, to make sure everyone was on the same page. I was brought in there at the end so they could discuss it all with me. Of course, I broke down as I heard them talk about how sick she was and how long this would take.

The plan is that she needs both physical therapy and dialysis every day. Those are her biggest issues right now: acute kidney injury and overall muscle wasting/ weakness.

Of course, the kidney issue is really starting to worry me. I know I shouldn't worry, but that's really hard for a mom to not do, especially in our situation. I fluctuate between worry and strong confidence every day. I know God is in control. I'd just like Him to control it my way if that could be possible. But, I'm trusting in who He says He is... loving, good, mighty, all-powerful, sovereign, righteous, faithful, Provider, and ALWAYS Healer.

Over that year, Katie bounced back and forth from PICU to the bone marrow transplant floor. Any time she would have a bleed or need 24-hour dialysis, she would have to be in PICU. At this point, Katie had been doing well on hemodialysis three to four times a week and was continuing to produce urine. I continued to hold out hope that her kidneys would make a full recovery once all this bleeding got under control, despite what all the renal doctors told me.

In early July 2016, Katie ended up back in the ICU due to yet another GI bleed. She seemed to be stuck in the pattern of bleeding, healing, getting stronger, then starting over with bleeding again. We had been in and out of the PICU five times in four weeks. While we loved the PICU staff, we were growing pretty weary. We wanted our girl stable enough to not have to be there.

Because Katie's bleeding hadn't stopped after a couple of days, the GI doctors decided they should go in, once again, for another upper and lower scope. On that Tuesday at 1:00 pm, our girl was rolled to the operating room for her sixth scope, a pretty simple procedure. The doctors always had to be very careful because her tissue was so fragile and inflamed.

We waited for the doctors to come out with their pictures and to tell us what they found, just like they always did. They walked into the waiting room about thirty minutes after the procedure started. This couldn't be good. I thought they obviously weren't able to see anything.

The doctors ended up only performing an upper scope. When they looked into her stomach and the opening of her small intestine, they saw a hematoma... the same hematoma that had been there a couple of weeks ago when clips were inserted to close up a large, bleeding ulcer. The hematoma hadn't shrunk in size. The hope was that her body would absorb it over time. The doctor thought something was under the hematoma "feeding it"... a bleed. We would have to incorporate surgeons into a conversation on ways to clear the hematoma safely to see what was under there. The plan was to discuss over a day or two and decide.

Richard and I walked back to Katie's PICU room to wait for her to get rolled back. We hadn't even been sitting there five minutes when the surgery liaison came in to say the anesthesiologist wanted to speak to us in one of the family conference rooms. We headed over there thinking he was simply going to update us on what went on with her sedation.

The anesthesiologist told us that as he had pulled Katie's breathing tube out and they were getting ready to wheel her back to the room, they noticed her gown was soaked with blood on the right side of her chest. When they pulled her gown back, they saw a very large skin tear (it ended up being 6 cm x 20 cm). She'd had a few skin tears, but nothing of this magnitude. This was basically a large, open wound, not a small tear, that would be treated as a burn over the next months with excruciatingly painful dressing changes every single day until it started to heal.

They called for plastic surgery to come and look at it before they put a dressing on it. As they were waiting, Katie began vomiting lots of blood. They quickly put the breathing tube back in because they did not want any blood to get into her lungs.

As he was telling us this, the GI team came back into the room, accompanied by the chief of surgery and our BMT doctor. A decision had to be made. Our precious girl was lying there on the operating table waiting for what would come next. Something had to be done.

We had two choices: either continue down the path we were on where she faced a life-threatening incident every week or two, or go in and clean out this area and see if there was a bleed under this hematoma by an artery or something that could be fixed.

We asked a lot of questions, we discussed all the options, and ultimately we agreed with our BMT doctor, who said we needed to do what we could do now. One of these incidents, if they continued like this, could cause her death. We decided that, if she were going to bleed, then it would be safer for her to bleed on the operating

128

table where it could be managed better rather than in the PICU room or room on any other floor.

The surgeon said it was a "very high-risk" procedure and would be considered "emergency surgery." The GI doctor would go in one more time, endoscopically, to see if she could see anything behind the hematoma and possibly try to clear it out, while the surgeons stood by to intervene.

Richard said one more thing before the doctors left to see our girl. He said, "I don't know what your faith is and what you believe, but we are people of faith. Would you mind if we prayed with you before you go in?" They accepted. With tears streaming down his face, he thanked God for them and prayed that God would give them guidance during this procedure. He also reminded God of how much Katie loved Him and that we knew He was a good Father who wanted good things for her. The doctors shook our hands and headed to the OR. Richard and I went back to Katie's room to wait. We sat in silence. We cried. We prayed.

Another 45 minutes later, the surgeon and the GI doctor walked into our rooms, smiling. They said, "Good news!" I breathed a huge sigh of relief.

The GI doctor was able to see the source of the bleed because Katie had apparently vomited up the hematoma and the blood that had covered it. Where the clips had been placed, there was an area that was just dripping blood, like a leaky faucet. She cleared the way for them to see the bleed endoscopically after all. No "emergency" surgery was needed. We thanked God for that because, with all her bleeding issues, "opening her up," at that point would not have been a good option.

It was not the day we expected, but also not a day with which we'd been unfamiliar. We had experienced several life-threatening times with our girl. Scary moments. Moments no parent should ever have to experience. We prayed this would be the last of these moments.

I've come to realize that you can scared and trust God at the same time. Sometimes life is just scary. We know our God is always for us and loves us dearly, and we throw all our trust in Him during these scary times. Scripture says, "When I am afraid, I will trust in You." (Psalm 56:3) It's not *if* I am afraid, it's *when*. That means there *will* be times when we are going to be afraid and have fear. What's important is how we respond to it. We must bring our fears to God, lay them at His feet, and trust.

THIS GIRL, PART TWO
Richard

*She was powerful, not because she wasn't scared, but because she
went on so strongly, despite the fear.*
- Harper Lee, *To Kill a Mockingbird*

From Day One, Katie saw something that, perhaps, we didn't. We were fighting to save her life. We were running around, trying to find solutions and cures. We were frantically trying to find meaning in all of the sorrow and sickness. She was trying to honor God.

Even from my first conversation with her about what was happening, she showed a level of maturity that I have not seen in many people who have served God much longer than her.

Even through the most laborious, grueling, frightful, tiring, painful, isolating circumstances, Katie remained a true champion. She's the reason you are reading this book, for without her incredible spirit, there would be no story to tell.

Maybe that was her plan all along—to have a story worth telling. And that is what this chapter is all about. I want to give you a tiny peek into the person Katie was, after her diagnosis. The following examples are mere glimpses of her incredible character, love, strength, and honorable nature. When she could have turned bitter (and no one would have blamed her for it), she clothed herself in God's character and nature. It, truly, was the most beautiful thing I've ever seen.

Rewind to the beginning of all this, to the time we had just gotten home from her first ER and hospital visit, right after her initial, preliminary diagnosis. As I was putting her to bed that night, we began to talk about all that was happening. We talked about her hospital stay, her doctor, her friends who came to visit, and a few other things surrounding the previous week.

I asked her a simple question, one that I would continue to ask throughout her ordeal, getting a different, but equally amazing answer each time.

"Katie, what do you think about all this?"

"Daddy, I just want what brings God the most glory, even if it results in my own death."

This simple reply to a simple question became the impetus for the way we would spend the rest of Katie's life, how we would treat the situation, how we would view everything surrounding her illness and treatment. It would become the filter through which every decision and conversation passed.

As she moved along her journey towards transplant, as weird as it sounds, whole worlds, the likes of which we never considered, opened up to us and to her. We went from a normal family to routinely discussing bone marrow issues, treatments, recovery, and all sorts of things into which our new life would thrust us.

When I was initially at Texas Children's Hospital for her transplant, Katie was afforded the opportunity to take part in a survey about teenagers going through stem cell transplants. Each time she took the survey, she would earn ten dollars. One of the questions on the very first survey was something to the effect of, "Do you ever just wish this would've never happened?"

Of course, *my* answer would have been, "Ummmm... yeah."

But, her answer was this: "Well, no, because obviously God has something He's going to do through this, and use me in some way."

Again, a simple reply, but profoundly sure of God's will and working in her life.

A few weeks later, in her hospital room during her transplant stay, she watched a wedding on TV. Up until this point, she hadn't shown very much emotion, but when she saw that wedding, it opened up a flood of things she'd been carrying.

This is Daphne's journal entry, dated August 31, 2015:

Katie finally had a breakdown of her own emotions. We'd been waiting for it. Sure, there'd been tears here and there, but nothing like this. She sobbed, uncontrollably, for over an hour. She expressed so many things to me that she was feeling, and at one point, cried over the fact that maybe she hasn't been a good "Christian witness" to her friends. Her heart broke at the fact that her friends might go to hell. Wow.

It made me think about myself and when was the last time I sobbed over some of my own friends who don't know Jesus. That, I don't even remember.

She cried about how her friends are consumed with unimportant things right now like popularity and boys and how that's SO not important. There are a lot of friends who have abandoned her at this point. I explained that people do love her and care for her, for all of us, but they have their own lives and this is a great lesson in friendship for her at such a young age. She will truly know what a good friend looks like and how to be one.

Because let me tell y'all something, there is not one thing fake or phony about her. What you see is what you get, like it or not. And, she is the BEST friend anyone could ask for.

She also cried about wanting to get married, see her sister married and have children, and not ever wanting her parents to lose a child. It was an amazing conversation I got to have with her.

I was able to speak the truth of God's Word to her... that He has a plan and a future for her. Always had. Always will.

After that late conversation, she got the best night's sleep she's ever had in the hospital. It was a great release off of her. The things she spoke in that conversation were some heavy things to carry deep inside. We prayed and were immediately surrounded by the peace of God. It was a great night's sleep for both of us!

A month after she was readmitted for graft versus host disease, Katie and Daphne were reading a daily devotional about being thankful. Daphne asked her if she found it hard to thank God "in all circumstances," considering her own situation at that time.

Her reply? "No. I can easily thank God for anything." She proceeded to start thanking God for things that day, that she got to drink water, that she wasn't as nauseous as the day before, and several other things that we often take for granted.

Another thing we began to notice about her was her complete selflessness and concern for others. Here's Daphne's journal entry from February 25th, 2016:

Yesterday marked nine days in which Katie has been in pain. Some days are worse than others, but yesterday seemed to me more manageable than the rest.

However, some intense pain hit her in the early evening. It was the worst of the day.

In that moment, she grabbed my hand and said, "Can we pray?"

This is not uncommon for her to do. She asks quite frequently when her pain is pretty severe and we will immediately pray for relief and strength.

But this time was different.

In this particular moment, she didn't ask to pray for herself at all, despite her pain level being high. She said this: "Can we pray for Mrs. Kindra, Anais, and Paige? I want to pray that no one ever has to go through this and they would never have to experience how hard this is." (ed. note: The people she asked to pray for are people who were about to or were going through transplants. Kindra is recovering, and Anais and Paige are with Katie in Heaven). She admitted "this is so hard." We already knew this, but to hear her say it makes it even harder.

She cried at the thought of them experiencing the pain she has been in. I cried. It was another precious moment where I was able to see inside my girl's heart. She has ALWAYS had a huge heart for people and shown compassion for those who are hurting.

This girl continues to amaze me. She has gone through and continues to go through more hard stuff than most people will ever experience in their lives. We are all ready for her to get real relief and move forward in her healing process.

One night, in April 2016, as Daphne was about to leave for her last women's conference as the church's women's ministry director, we had a real sweet conversation with Katie.

She'd had some pretty intense nausea all day and, by the end of the day, had vomited quite a bit of blood again. As you can imagine, that situation would prove to be quite scary for all of us.

As we tucked her into bed, she began to cry. She looked at us, through tears, and said, "I love you so much. I just want y'all to know how much I really love y'all."

We told her we loved her, too, and that we knew she loved us.

She said, "I feel like I have taken life for granted. We don't know what tomorrow holds and I want to make sure y'all know that. I haven't told you enough how much I love you. I want to tell you a lot every day."

I tried to encourage her, reminding her that she still had a lot of life to live. She agreed, and said she'd continue to fight, no matter how long it took.

A few days later, while Daphne was at her conference, it was just Katie and me at the hospital. Bear in mind that, at this point, her body was covered in scars and stretch marks from the high-dose steroid treatments. She was completely swollen from head to toe and needed help walking and going to the bathroom. Because of that, she was long-since over the idea of her daddy seeing her naked. As we sat in the bathroom, she on the toilet, and me on the edge of the tub, we had another conversation in which I got to see who Katie was on the inside.

Looking at her scars and stretch marks was always difficult for me, but she never really said anything about them. That night, I decided to ask.

"I'm so sorry this has happened to you. You know that, if I could have done anything about this, I would have, right?"

"Yes, Daddy."

"And your skin. Those scars. I'm so sorry. What do you think about this?"

She raised her head, but didn't look directly at me, and said perhaps the most profound thing I've ever heard in my entire life:

"Daddy, Jesus has His scars, and I have mine."

She was only fifteen years old at the time, but the maturity and depth of that response belied her youth. I was instantly convicted of my own selfishness. I remember thinking, "I get upset when the red light doesn't change to green fast enough."

There were no words I could offer her at that point. My baby girl possessed an insight into God's character that I may never achieve. I was completely torn apart by the pain of those words while equally amazed at her incredible depth.

Even on heavy medication, Katie continued to amaze us with how much she understood God's character and Word.

This is Daphne's journal entry from May 24, 2016:

Yesterday morning, I leaned over my baby girl and kissed her forehead. I hugged her as much as I could hug her over all the lines attached to her body. And I said what I say every day to her, "You are an amazing girl. I love you."

Then I said, "I am also amazed at how hard you are fighting this and not giving up."

She said to me, "It's because of you."

I said, "What do you mean?"

And my sweet, pain-med-induced girl said this: "It's what you always taught me... Train up a child in the way she should go and when she is old she will not depart from it."

Tears streamed down my face.

If you only knew how much pain medication my girl is on, you would appreciate even more the fact that she could quote Scripture. Most people can't quote a verse fully lucid.

To again say how amazing she is just isn't enough.

We've seen how simply pure-hearted this girl is through this whole process. People say lots of stuff on pain meds, usually not good stuff. Everything that has come out of our girl has been pure... at times, frustrated and angry... but always pure. Richard and I are just in awe of her and her faith.

She was always ready to bring God into the mix. She was always giving Him glory in her situation. She was always showing me how to respond correctly to life's most difficult challenges. Somewhere about mid-June 2016, during her longest stint in PICU (around two months, actually), she went on and off the ventilator a couple of times. On the second time around, as soon as the tube was out, she began crying, and said, "I'm so happy. God is my healer." It was pretty amazing. She then said, "God is my healer," several times after that.

Even in the midst of the suffering, we kept seeing incredible glimpses of Katie's strength, love, and kindness. During some of her physical therapy sessions, her assignment was to get into a wheelchair and take a ride through the bone marrow unit. It was not enough for Katie simply to ride in a wheelchair. She asked us to purchase Hershey's Kisses and other small candies so that she could pass them out to nurses, doctors, support staff, other parents, and anyone else on the floor. This process happened several times, and it became affectionately known as Katie's reverse trick-or-treating.

There was one physical therapy session that still stands out in my mind. After Katie became somewhat proficient in wheeling herself around, the next step was to get her to stand again. Once she could master standing, we would move on to her being able to take baby steps with a walker, and eventually get around without one. We were in the bone marrow unit's game room, and her physical therapist was trying to get her to stand up and sit back down. Katie would have to place her hands on the therapist's shoulders or lower back, as a support while trying to stand. They did that a couple of times, and then Katie asked if she could do it with me. Of course, I obliged. I helped her stand a couple of times, and then the therapist asked Katie to stay standing and just shift side to side. Katie struggled with lifting her feet to make the shifts happen, and her therapist had to explain it to her a couple of times. All of a sudden, Katie said, "Oh, kinda like dancing!"

"Yes! Exactly like dancing!"

At that point, she looked up at me, put her hands up on my shoulders, began singing a song that I didn't recognize, and she began dancing, bidding me to join her. In that moment, although, because of the high-dose steroids, my baby girl looked like a whole other person, I saw my Katie. I saw that beautiful girl who loved to dance, who loved to sing, who loved to be sweet to her daddy. It's a memory I'll never forget. It's a memory I've worked diligently to preserve. We danced so many dances before then, but this one has become the most special to me.

For her sixteenth birthday, she wrote individual invitations to her nurses to come by her room. In the invitations, she stated, "no presents." When asked why she wrote that, she said it was because they already had done so much for her, and that she just wanted to bless them. She wanted to give everyone cupcakes, so, in true Katie reverse trick-or-treat fashion, her physical therapy session that day consisted of her getting into the wheelchair to roll around the unit to hand out goodie bags to all the staff!

One of the most beautiful acts of selflessness on her part came during the Christmas season of 2016. Katie was really upset that she was still in the hospital, even with Kylie's impending arrival for the holiday. She felt it would ruin Kylie's trip (Katie always wanted everyone to be happy and not burdened with her situation).

When she and I were in the dialysis unit for her normal dialysis time, there was an organization handing out presents. One lady asked Katie what she wanted. She said she didn't want anything. The lady continued to insist she choose something, pulling out all kinds of gifts she might like. Katie still said she didn't want anything. Finally, after the lady pressed her, she chose an art set.

We already had about six art sets, some new, and some with pieces missing (because that's how those things seem to always end up), so I was wondering why she would choose *another* one, since art wasn't something that even held her interest.

Again, a simple response revealing her incredible character: "Kylie would like that. I'm going to give it to her."

In April 2017, we were finally able to go to church as a family for the first time since December 2015. For many people, not attending church for a year and a half isn't even a thing, but Katie was practically born on a church pew. Again, with both parents on staff at a church, it had become a very large part of who she was.

Obviously, it felt great for all of us to be in church as a family. Katie sat in her wheelchair, in the handicapped area, with Daphne to her immediate left and me to the left of Daphne. During the third worship song, I looked down as Daphne was bending over Katie in her wheelchair. Katie's was holding her head in her hands and she was sobbing. Daphne sat down and held her. When Daphne asked her why she was crying, her response was, "It just feels so good to be in church again."

Again, something so simple, yet profound. What we all take for granted, and some even spurn, she saw as precious.

In July of 2017, I had planned a trip to see Kylie in Australia. This was my second attempt, with my first being thwarted by an unexpected hospital admission on the night of Thanksgiving 2016. Things were all set for my second trip, but then came Katie's last PICU visit—the one she would never leave. I was still set to go until the day she had the first large GI bleed. At that point, I knew I had to cancel. I called Kylie and told her what was happening, and of course she understood. Now I just had to let Katie know.

Katie was sedated so that her team could install a breathing tube and insert a femoral IV line and a couple other peripheral lines. When she came to, I informed her I was staying. Immediately, she got a sad look on her face, and started mouthing the name "Kylie." Even in the midst of her situation, she was thinking of her sister. The following exchange shows just how incredible her love for her sister was, matched by her own selflessness.

"Baby, Kylie will be okay. You need me here, and so does your mother."

More mouthing of the name "Kylie" and shaking her head.

"No, Baby. I'm staying. I've already cancelled my flight."

She then motioned for a piece of paper and a pen. Once they were given, she then wrote the sweetest four words.

"You need to go."

I am beyond thankful for a daughter who was so gracious, loving, kind, and faith-filled. She embodied selflessness and sweetness. I am so proud to be her daddy.

STRETCH MARKS
Daphne

Life with [God] is not immunity *from* difficulties, but
peace *in* difficulties.
- Anonymous, *God Calling*

This morning, I was thankful for the five minutes I had before my alarm rang. I loathe the sound of an alarm. It doesn't matter what time the alarm is set for, I just hate it. I'd much rather wake up naturally. That's why this morning was more pleasant. I got out of bed with less effort and was happy that I would have five more minutes to enjoy a cup of coffee before heading to the gym. These last few years I haven't been able to take care of myself like I was used to, and hospital life can help pack on the pounds. I gained twenty-five pounds through that time, so unfortunately, the gym has become a must these days.

I made my way to the bathroom, stepped out of my pajamas, and proceeded to grab my workout clothes from our walk-in closet. As I walked by the full-length mirror, leaning up against the bathroom wall, I caught a glimpse of myself. I paused, turned to the side, and tried to hold my stomach in like I figure everyone does when they walk by a mirror. Maybe it's just me. But, this time, my eyes were fixed on the stretch marks put there by the wonderful progression of pregnancy. And, this time, I didn't cringe when I saw them.

Instead, I thought about Katie.

As I write this, she's been gone for just over three months now. I am struggling just to make it through each day. The thoughts and memories of her are a constant in my mind. I thought about how my pregnancy with Katie caused these stretch marks. I had none with Kylie.

I was always so worried about getting rid of them, but though they have faded over time, those stretch marks are different to me now. I love them. I embrace them. I don't want them to fade any further. They serve as a constant reminder of how I carried that sweet, beautiful girl in my body for nine months. They remind me of how late she was, which is how I got those stretch marks to begin with. She was late. Very late, as I mentioned in the prologue.

The wait for her arrival seemed like forever. And, in that waiting time, as it got closer to the end, I was miserable. I just kept getting bigger and bigger. I wasn't a cute, little pregnant woman anymore. Think of Violet Beauregarde, the gum-chewing girl who turned into a giant, rotund blueberry in the movie *Willy Wonka and the Chocolate Factory*, and you should have a pretty good picture of how this was going. I was enormous, barely able to move. After the attempted induction, I was done and just wanted her out. Enough was enough.

The longer I had to wait, the more stretch marks developed. The funny thing is, during my pregnancy I didn't even see the stretch marks because they were on the underside of my belly, which, of course, I couldn't see. Despite all the cocoa-butter rubbing, there was no preventing these suckers. After Katie finally showed up a few weeks later (on her own, mind you, and in her own time… no induction necessary), I discovered that all the cocoa butter in the world would never get rid of the caverns she left behind.

In the waiting, I grew. As I grew, stretch marks became more evident, even when they weren't visible to me. I didn't always handle the waiting well. I complained. I cried. I was anxious. I wanted it all done on my timetable. When the waiting was over, I had a beautiful outcome. But there were marks left behind that remind me of the time I spent waiting. Instead of trying to hide those marks, I now embrace them as reminders of the journey. They aren't pretty, but they tell a beautiful story.

The outcome of our wait over the years when Katie was sick doesn't seem beautiful to me. If I'm being honest, I hate the outcome. I wanted her healed *here*. But that's not how God chose to heal her. The marks left behind by waiting for her healing are deeper than any stretch mark or scar could ever be. But I'm working on embracing those marks and finding the beauty in them. This was my journal entry on May 31, 2016, written during one of Katie's long stints in PICU:

Waiting is exhausting. My entire day is centered around waiting. I wake up and wait. I wait until the time I go to bed. Then I wake up and do the same thing all over again.

I wait on doctors.
I wait on procedures.
I wait on tests.
I wait on results.
I wait on good news.
I wait on a breakthrough.
I wait for a good day.
I wait for healing.

149

It is exhausting.

Even when I sleep, I wake up exhausted. My eyes hurt. My body is tired despite the fact that I sit all day. I sit and wait.

I always knew waiting was never easy. This is not the first time I've had to wait in my life. Waiting just seems to be a part of life... a huge part of life. I just never knew how much it could consume a life.

Obviously this whole process has aged me. I look in the mirror and don't recognize who I see. I'm tired and old. Each day seems to age me six months.

I've been so thankful for some good nights of uninterrupted sleep and a few hours to get a break out of the hospital each day thanks to my parents being here. It's been incredible having help. I always knew having someone here to help would have been huge, but now that I've had it for a few weeks, I'm convinced it's vital. Sad thing is that my parents leave tomorrow and I'm back to doing the majority of this hospital stuff on my own since Richard has to work. Thinking of my parents being gone just made me even more tired.

Katie is tired, more tired than ever. She's been stuck in PICU for almost a month. Her spirits are pretty low. She's sad and feels isolated from everyone, even her "eighth-floor family" (as she called them). Lying in bed for almost a month in the same room can be quite depressing. She continues to work with physical therapy when she can and definitely needs to build her strength back up to get out of the bed.

We are waiting for that breakthrough that w
back to the eighth floor and the even bigger t
that will send us home.

I'm hanging on to this Scripture and trusting the Lord for
strength just to get through each day: Those who trust in
(wait on) the Lord will find new strength. (Isaiah
40:31a)

We all wait. We wait for answers to life's questions. Where do I go from here? God, what do you want me to do? Am I ever going to get out of this situation? Will I ever be free of this? How will you use me?

It's in the waiting that we grow. We grow in our faith and our relationship with God. We grow in maturity and in wisdom. In that growth, marks and scars form. It's just part of life. We make mistakes and wrestle with decisions. How we respond determines how many marks are left behind. But others can also make marks upon us, and we have to deal with them all the same.

How awesome would it be if we could embrace our marks, our scars, our wounds in all their ugliness? We all have some pretty ugly marks, gained through times of struggle, that we try to hide. But those marks were never meant to be hidden; they're meant to be embraced. They serve as reminders of our own journey... mistakes, tragedy, disaster, affliction, trauma, trial—all of it.

Embrace your stretch marks. They may not be pretty, but
they tell a beautiful story.

In the waiting, we become anxious. We're always looking forward to the next thing. As kids, we can't wait

151

to grow up. We can't wait to finish school. We can't wait to get married. We can't wait to have children. We can't wait for all kinds of things. Even more... We wait for God's answer on all kinds of decisions and on His guidance.

Where will He lead us? What will He have us do? We wait for healing to be complete. We wait for heartache to heal. We wait for opportunities to open up for us. We wait for finances to finally be in our favor.

The fact is, there will be times in our lives when we will have to wait. No doubt about it. It's inevitable. So the question becomes: *How* will we wait?

I am learning how to wait well. Waiting well is hard. It includes praise in times of sadness. It includes faith in place of doubt. It includes a heart full of great expectation in the face of bad news. It includes lots of real conversations with God in place of cookie-cutter prayers. It includes tons of trust in God, His character, and His Word when you feel like your world is collapsing around you.

I'm still in the waiting. I'm still learning how to wait well. I fail at times—many times—because I want to control the direction of things. Let's face it, waiting is hard. We want answers and we want them now. A lot of times, the answers we seek feel crucial to our lives and the lives of others, and having to wait just doesn't make sense. I remind myself that God sees it all. He sees everything we can't see. And if we have to wait, then there *must* be something good in store for us on the other side.

I'm realizing that it's in the waiting not that God is most present, but that *I* am most present. I hear God more clearly... mainly because I'm listening more closely. In the waiting, we must remember that God has not left us, but is in it the whole time. God is the same in the

waiting as He is in the contentment and the victc
is always present, always working for our good.

Waiting is never wasted when you're w:
God. He always proves His faithfulness. "GOD proves to
be good to the man who passionately waits, to the
woman who diligently seeks. It's a good thing to quietly
hope, quietly hope for help from GOD." (Lamentations
3:25-26)

We wait well by knowing and trusting the
character of God. You want to wait well? You want to
wait with no fear, no anxiety? Know who God is. That
only happens through studying His Word. Learn His
character.

He is trustworthy.

*Those who know your name, trust in You, for You, Lord, have never
forsaken those who seek You.*
- Psalm 9:10 (NIV)

Throughout the Bible, we see story after story of
God coming through for people, just as He promised,
even when situations looked dire. The walls of Jericho
fell. Water came out of the rock for Moses. Sarah got
pregnant. The Israelites were freed. The lions spared
Daniel. On and on and on we could go.

I'm sure all of these instances and more were
faced with some doubt. Our eyes can deceive us when
we're trying to trust God. But the thing that all these
people have in common is that they trusted God despite
their circumstances.

153

I wish I could tell you it's easy. It sometimes is, especially after a victory or answered prayer. But in the thick of it, trust can be hard.

When all this started for us with Katie, the song "Oceans" by Hillsong United was very popular and sung in church constantly. I loved the song. Everyone loved the song. I sang it with wild abandon…

> *Spirit, lead me where my trust is without borders*
> *…take me deeper than my feet could ever wander*
> *where my faith will be made stronger*

I sang this for years. I firmly believe we shouldn't sing songs to God that we aren't willing to back up with our lives. The same thing goes for our prayers. If we're going to say, "God, use me," then we better be prepared for doors to open to whatever area He chooses, and then we should be prepared to say, "Yes," and walk through them.

As this life change punched us in the gut, I always thought about that particular line …*Spirit, lead me where my trust is without borders…* as I sang it in church, and especially as I led thousands of people in singing it with me. I contemplated what that really meant and whether I actually wanted that. Did they realize what they were singing with me? What does "trust without borders" mean? It means I can say with my *whole* heart, "God, I trust You in *everything*!"

It's easy to pick and choose which areas we can give to God and trust Him with. That's trusting God *with* borders… giving over certain areas, but then holding tightly to others. We like to keep control of those areas. Because then we don't have to make ourselves vulnerable to hurt. We keep it to ourselves to protect ourselves. It's human nature. Protection of self is part of what we do.

When we sing that line, we should be prep
for whatever may come our way. That's a *huge* statemειι
to sing! Do you realize what you're saying to God? You're
asking God to take you to a level where you can trust
Him completely with anything and everything that will
come your way.

Throughout Katie's ordeal, God brought that
lyric to my remembrance, over and over again.
"Remember what you said? Remember what you sang?
Here's your chance to trust Me more, without borders, in
everything." And, that's exactly what I attempted to do in
all this.

It's what I still pursue: trust without borders. To
say to God, "No matter what, I will trust You. Even
when I don't understand, I will trust You." I know God
doesn't cause things like we experienced; however, He
definitely walked with us in it and always had a purpose
through it. As this journey unfolded, He drew close to us.
He taught us. And we *had* to trust Him more.

As I prayed for different things through those
years, God would bring those lyrics to me again: *Spirit,
lead me where my trust is without borders.* I realized, in my
prayers, I was putting God in a box (borders) and saying
the only way Katie could be healed was either
miraculously through God's hand or naturally through a
perfect bone marrow match transplant. But God showed
me that He could heal her any way He wanted, through
any means—and that it may not be the way I wanted.

I gave up control and prayed differently: "God...
whatever way You want to heal her, I'm good with that.
It doesn't matter to me. You heal the way You desire to
heal her." Her healing definitely did not come the way I
desired. But the fact remains that she is healed.

We can trust without borders. We can trust who
God is. We can trust He knows best. We can just trust...
because He is trustworthy.

He is our strength.

But he said to me, "My grace is sufficient for you, for my power is made perfect in weakness."
- 2 Corinthians 12:9a (NIV)

I always got a little perturbed when people would tell Katie or me to "be strong" or commend us for being "so strong" through this time. It's way too much pressure to put on someone going through situations like this to tell them to "be strong." I just want to say right back, "You be strong, because I just can't right now." Of course, that wouldn't have been real Christian of me to say, so I always held my tongue.

Honestly, I am not strong and I was not strong. Not at all. I didn't want to be strong. It's exhausting. I think that's the reason why God doesn't want us to "be strong." Relying on our own strength just doesn't cut it.

At the start of this journey, Katie had so many people telling her how strong she was and how strong she was going to be through this. Because of this, she internalized a narrative and bottled up most of her emotions about what was happening to her. She rarely cried and if there were tears, they were brief... usually about not being able to go to an event because of her diagnosis. Really, no emotions at all through the start of this journey.

She spent a long time at the beginning of our hospital time being straight-faced and all her answers were shoulder shrugs. I wondered what was going on inside her head and her heart. I even suggested she talk to one of the counselors. Nope. She didn't want to do that either. Apparently, she thought her daddy and I were good enough. She really didn't want to talk about

156

everything going on. We read our devotionals at night. We prayed. I asked how she was doing, how she was feeling. Again: shoulder shrugs. She was "being strong."

Then there was the first breakdown. This was after her transplant happened. She cried for about an hour and a half, and they had to give her Benadryl to calm her down. I had never seen anything like it. But it needed to happen. All of those bottled-up feelings and emotions came rolling out. I thought that was it.

But once she opened that door, the emotions kept flowing. It was actually a beautiful thing. She had really been so focused on trying to "be strong" this whole time like everyone was telling her to do, but even strong girls break sometimes.

Actually, they need to break. We all do.

We can be as strong as we possibly can, but to no avail. There will be a breaking point. There has to be. There were times I would take a moment away from the hospital and head out to run at a nearby track. It was my alone time. It became precious to me. I spent most of those runs crying. Although my body was trucking along, my heart was breaking. I would pray. I would worship. I would call out to God. The other runners had to think I was a lunatic as they passed me while I sobbed, barely breathing, not only from the running alone, but also from the painful surrender in my heart.

I ran in a broken state. That's how most of us "run" every day. Broken. Trying to be strong. The difference is, I couldn't be strong through this. I clung to Jesus like I never have before. I was the picture of weak.

There were moments in the hospital room where Katie would be sleeping, and in the darkness, I would break. I would cry. I would pray. I would call out to God again.

There was no one who could help me. No words could really make a difference. I only had Jesus. I only

ιope God had given me. I only had His Word
promises. They were the only things that
any kind of strength. But most of all, there
ny moments of peace. I would pray for God's
peace to dwell in that hospital room with us. When I was
broken, I felt the arms of a mighty God and good Father
holding me.

God's desire is not for us to be strong. God wants
us to rely on *Him* for strength. We cannot do it on our
own. It just doesn't work and, like I said, it's exhausting.
You can go ahead and keep on trying, but it simply will
not work forever. Just like my sweet girl broke, you will
too.

It's in your moments of brokenness, moments of
weakness, moments of fear, that God comes in and holds
you up. When you draw near to Him, He's there.
Always. I have truly been living out "in my weakness, I
am strong (He is strong)."

In other words, I am weak. Yep, I said it. I'm
going to own those words. Many Christ-followers would
never utter those words. They see those words as "a
negative confession."

I learned from the best about positive and
negative confessions when I spent my years in Tulsa,
Oklahoma, attending a few mega-churches and finishing
up my degree at Oral Roberts University. Tulsa seemed
like the capital for name-it, claim-it teachings and
declarations.

The thinking was that we "call things which are
not as though they were" (Romans 4:17) and *never* say
anything negative, professing weakness and the like...
never ever. Someone might hear us, I guess. Or worse, the
devil might hear us! Like he doesn't already know that
we're weak so we can fool him with our positive words
about ourselves.

Are they really simply positive words or lies?

There's a difference between stating who God says we are in His Word and simple lies. There was a time when I bought into all this, but the last few years have taught me something different.

I remember, years ago, as I was leading a certain worship song in church, that there was some disagreement about the lyrics. The lyrics stated, "I'm so weak and You're so strong," and went on to proclaim how God lifts us up and gives us strength. We actually changed the lyrics so as not to sing the words, "I'm so weak." I didn't understand that at the time. I didn't see what the big deal was in saying that I was weak. Because I am. I still don't understand the logic in it now.

Truth is: I *am* weak. Denying that fact just makes me a liar. It's *only* through Christ that I have any strength at all. We can say whatever we want, but that doesn't change the truth.

Paul said it best...

Each time he said, "My grace is all you need. My power works best in weakness." So now I am glad to boast about my weaknesses, so that the power of Christ can work through me. That's why I take pleasure in my weaknesses, and in the insults, hardships, persecutions, and troubles that I suffer for Christ. For when I am weak, then I am strong. - 2 Corinthians 12:9-10 (NLT)

It seems that Paul actually "boasted" in his weaknesses. That's how God shows His strength through us... in our weakness. If we don't claim to be weak, then how is God glorified?

I would still catch myself correcting Katie when she would say she "felt sick" or she said she "was sick." I would say, "Don't say that." But the truth was that *she was sick*. Saying that didn't negate the fact that Jesus paid the price for her healing. Saying that didn't negate the fact that she was healed. Saying that didn't give the enemy any more power. Saying that simply meant that it's Jesus who sustained her and made her strong through this.

Instead of boasting about how strong we are, we should be boasting in our weakness, giving God the glory for His strength, which is what upholds us. I understand the power in our words and I'm not saying we should be proclaiming negative things about ourselves, because those would be lies. We should still speak truth about who we are as God's children, but let's not try to hide the fact that we have struggles. It creates this negative perception of who Christ-followers are. We are not perfect people, not in the least.

Proclaim who you are: loved, cherished, heir with Christ, blessed, the righteousness of God, redeemed, forgiven, free, chosen, an overcomer. Say those things because they are true. But, let's not deceive ourselves into thinking we aren't weak, that we don't struggle with all kinds of things like sickness. We can boast in those, always remembering and proclaiming that it's God who makes us strong. We literally have nothing to do with it.

Now, when people say the words, "You're so strong," to me, my response is, "No, I'm actually not." That is the time I can boast in my weakness and give God the glory by letting people know that any semblance of strength they see only comes from God. It's *only* Jesus who picks us up, holds us up, and keeps us standing.

He is good.

You are good, and what you do is good…

- Psalm 119:68a (NIV)

Life can be hard. Actually, life *is* hard. There will be hard moments and seasons in your life. I have no doubt about that because Jesus even said we would have troubles in this world. It's pretty much a given. And just when you think something like this or worse can't happen to you or your family, it does. These things change you. They change everyone close to you. It can change you in a way where you grow and learn from it. Or it can change you in a not-so-good way, where you become angry and bitter, and turn your back on God.

Here's the truth: there are definitely some places in my heart that have been hurt through this. I wake up some mornings and ask God to make things not hurt and, most of all, not allow hurt to turn into bitterness. I ask God to make all of the hard things change me for good, to make me a better person, to allow me to be a part of the bigger plan in this.

But there are also some amazing moments that I hold close in my heart, that I go back to and thank God for, that I recall when my heart gets heavy. God's done some awesome things and I know He will continue. We must recall those things when life gets tough. Remember those things God has done for you. Meditate on them and thank Him for His goodness, His blessings. God's character never changes even though our life does. He is good even when our life is not or our life gets really hard.

Suffering doesn't negate God's goodness.

He's good, no matter what. That's just one of the many things God has shown me in this. Knowing God's character makes trusting Him a lot easier. He is good. The end. He can't do evil. It's not possible. This makes my love for Him even greater, knowing His plans would never be to harm any of His children. With all that said, I know that our lives will look different from here on out. We will never be "back to normal" again. We won't be. Life will be different, with new challenges. But no matter what we face, God's goodness remains.

He is the healer.

… and by His stripes we are healed.
- Isaiah 53:5b (NKJV)

At the start of this journey, I remember the doctor saying these exact words to us related to Katie's prognosis: "There are no guarantees." Those words weren't comforting to me at all. They rang over and over in my head: No guarantees.

Like most moms, I wanted a plan. A plan that would give us more of a guarantee, a plan that would help us have less anxiety and worry, a plan that would assure us that Katie would finally be rid of this illness and on her way back to a normal life. That's the kind of thing I wanted to hear. But that's not what we got. Instead, we got, "There are no guarantees."

Although it wasn't what I wanted to hear, it was the truth. There were no guarantees that any treatment would work. There were no guarantees Katie would beat this. And there are no guarantees for us in our lives here on this earth. None. There is only one guarantee: God, His promises, His Word. It's the *only* thing we can cling to or hold on to. Doctors can really only do so much. They do their best to help, to repair, but God is the *only one* who can guarantee us healing and life.

It's definitely burdensome to think about each day as not guaranteed for any of us, especially when it involves our children. To think when you wake up each morning that this day with the ones you love might be the last, or how you can make the most of each day, each moment. That's heavy stuff. It's definitely what I thought about each day. Thanking God for "this day" like we so often did in our daily prayers took on brand-new meaning for me. I cherished each day I had with Katie. And although her healing came in the form I didn't want, God still healed her.

I've heard preachers say from the pulpit, "God is moved by our faith, not by our need." I hate this statement. I get what they're trying to say, but it's not true. Or maybe I should say, it needs to be reworded. Maybe, "God is moved by our need, as we trust Him in faith." That sounds more like it to me.

Of course God is moved by our faith. But if God is a good Father, kind-hearted, loving, and compassionate, how can He *not* be moved by the needs of His children? Of course He is, just as an earthly father gives his child what they need. If his child were sick, he would do everything in his power to help that child—I speak from experience. I don't think any earthly father would *not* be moved by his child's needs, no matter what they may be. And I have to believe it's the same with our Heavenly Father. He is moved by our needs. He desires to meet them, especially when it comes to healing.

I get it. I understand that He is moved by our faith as we believe and trust Him. But God just had to look down from heaven on my sweet girl, as she spent years, struggling, fighting, suffering, hurting and be moved. He just had to. Just like I think He has to with every one of His children.

Jesus was moved by the needs of the people when He walked the earth. Look at the ways he treated people in Scripture:

And Jesus went about all Galilee, teaching in their synagogues, preaching the gospel of the kingdom, and healing all kinds of sickness and all kinds of disease among the people. Then his fame went throughout all Syria; and they brought Him all sick people who were afflicted with various diseases and torments, and those who were demon-possessed, epileptics, and paralytics; and He healed them.
—*Matthew 4:23-24 (NKJV)*

And He cast out the spirits with a word, and healed all who were sick, that it might be fulfilled which was spoken by Isaiah the prophet, saying: "He himself took our infirmities and bore our sicknesses."
—*Matthew 8:16-17 (NKJV)*

Then Jesus went about all the cities and villages, teaching in their synagogues, preaching the gospel of the kingdom, and healing every sickness and every disease among the people. But when He saw the multitudes, He was moved with compassion for them, because they were weary and scattered, like sheep having no shepherd.
—*Matthew 9:35-36 (NKJV)*

And when Jesus went out He saw a great multitude; and He was moved with compassion for them, and healed their sick.
—*Matthew 14:14 (NKJV)*

Now a leper came to Him, imploring Him, kneeling down to Him and saying to Him, "If you are willing, You can make me clean." Then Jesus, moved with compassion, stretched out His hand and touched him, and said to him, "I am willing; be cleansed."
—*Mark 1:40-41 (NKJV)*

He had compassion on them. He healed the He fed them. He was moved by their needs and met those needs. He healed every single person who asked for healing. The amount of faith these people had was this: they believed He could heal them. That's it. They didn't go through a big, super-spiritual ordeal to believe: It was simple. They were sick. They heard He could heal. They went to see Him. They believed. They were healed.

I could get into all the questions of why some believers get healed here on earth and some don't, but I won't. Obviously, because I don't know. No one does. I'm learning just to accept that some questions have no answers, because that's been my big question this whole time. However, it's useless for me to continue to ask a question to which I will never know the answer. I must accept the fact that God healed Katie in His way, not mine. I must continue to trust in God, that His ways are higher than mine, that He loves my family, that He sees us, and that, yes, He is moved by our needs and He always heals.

He is merciful.

The faithful love of the Lord never ends! His mercies never cease. Great is His faithfulness; His mercies are new every morning.
- Lamentations 3:22-23 (NLT)

That last line of these verses play over and over in my head. It's something we, as church-going people, hear all the time.

His mercies are new every morning.
New. Every. Morning.

Mercy is defined as "a blessing that is an act of divine favor or compassion." God grants us His divine favor and compassion every single day. These acts are specifically designed for us according to what we need that day. That's mind-blowing to me. God knows what we need before we need it, and His mercies are there waiting for us throughout the day.

Not the same mercies He extended to you yesterday. Or the day before. Or the day before that. And so on. And so forth.

His mercies are new. His mercies are the mercies you *need for that day*.

When I buy a new dress, it's one I've never worn before... one I've never used. It's brand new. It's the same with God's mercies. It's like putting on a new dress every day. He gives you mercies—not just a new mercy, but plural *mercies*. That's multiple dresses! Think of how many new mercies He bestows on us each day that we are not even aware of. His mercies are immeasurable. How many thousands of mercies has He given to us every day? New mercies, not old ones.

Every morning Katie was sick, my prayer was that God would grant us new mercies for that day... mercies for our sweet girl and her healing. He knew what she needed. He knew what *we* needed.

Her last week with us here on earth, I especially prayed this. I prayed for God's mercy to be upon her, as she so desperately fought for her life. I prayed for that act of compassion. He knew what mercy she needed at each moment, and ultimately, His great mercy was to take her home, healed and whole.

He offers grace.

Let us have confidence, then, and approach God's throne, where there is grace. There we will receive mercy and find grace to help us just when we need it.
- Hebrews 4:16 (GNT)

Not only does God grant us new mercies, but He also offers us grace.

Grace = Unmerited Favor

Each day in the hospital brought more problems and issues than resolutions and good reports. After over a year of that, a person can get worn down... or more like beaten down. After two years, I was a complete mess. When you live in that state, you feel as if someone might simply touch you and shatter you into a thousand pieces.

We've suffered a lot of loss. Not just losing our sweet girl, but also loss of family, loss of home, loss of friends. loss of jobs, loss of finances, loss of normalcy, loss of dreams, loss of goals, loss of just a good-old, plain, low-key life. I found myself in this shattered state most days, but with a smile on my face. No one knew. I stayed shattered.

But then... grace.

This is an excerpt from my journal entry on July 29th, 2016:

When I'm shattered, lying in these pieces on the floor, not able to produce the strength to stand, struggling to breathe, heart crumbling yet again... there is a grace that comes in.

It's not magic. It's grace.

It's a peace. That peace reminds me that God is carrying us. He won't stop carrying us.

And, each time I break, there's grace.

Grace isn't limited to a day.

God doesn't say, "Oh, sorry... you've reached the capacity of grace that you can have today." Some days I need more grace... grace upon grace upon grace. And He freely gives it to me.

When we get another bad report, bad news, something goes wrong... whatever the case may be, I try to take deep breaths, try to relax, listen to the doctors, but also try to drown out their voices with the voice of God, reminding me of His promises.

Sometimes those God-voices do get drowned out by the voices of others and words like "cancer" or "end-stage renal failure" or "she could die." That's when I break.

Sometimes I see my beautiful daughter, looking at herself in the mirror, cleaning her face for the day, staring, and crying at someone she doesn't recognize. Her heart breaks. She thinks she's ugly. She sees how people look at her. That's when I break even more.

When I break, His grace comes in and covers me.

I have this visual in my head of how my mom used to make the beds in the house, rolling and fluffing out this long blanket to cover it. Over and over again, the blanket would billow over the bed until it was finally perfectly covered, every inch underneath the blanket.

168

That's how I see grace. God billowing this grace blanket over me, over and over again, as many times as I need it, until every inch of me is covered... grace upon grace upon grace, whenever I need it.

There are definitely times we need more grace. God has shown us that His grace never runs out. Even though we have been walking through the darkest time in our lives, He has covered us. He goes before us. He prepares a way when we don't know how we're going to survive. We continue not to know what's ahead. We continue to trust. We continue to receive grace upon grace upon grace.

When we know who God really is and trust His character, we can be content in all things. *Contentment*: the word was so daunting to me in those trying days. I kept coming back to it over and over and over again... "be content, be content, be content." The definition of contentment, according to Merriam-Webster, is not what I have always perceived contentment to be. *Contentment: the state of being happy or satisfied.*

When I read this definition, it changes things for me. When I substitute that meaning in the line from Philippians 4:11 I had been wrestling with for those last few years, it becomes even more difficult to wrap my brain around.

... for I have learned how to be content with whatever I have.

Learning to be content with whatever I have. Whatever my circumstance, whatever life throws at me... that "whatever" has always been extremely difficult. I struggle with quieting my spirit, shushing my mind. But here, Paul says that whether he's in need, or in plenty, he has learned to be content in it.

I always thought being content was just being able to cope with a situation. That it was just not complaining and waiting it out quietly; I never imagined I was supposed to be *happy*, much less *satisfied* in it.

> *...for I have learned how to be* **happy** *with whatever I have.*
>
> *...for I have learned how to be* **satisfied** *with whatever I have.*

What a difference a word makes! I must confess that I was neither happy nor satisfied—and hadn't been for some time. I was most definitely the *opposite* of happy and satisfied. I didn't know how to be that. I could put on a good face, but inside I was filled with sadness. Still broken. Working as hard as I could to be content. I realized that this is an impossibility for me. It's totally possible when life is filled with blessings and life is good. But, I truly found this to be an impossible feat for me as I watched my child suffering for so long.

One night, my husband, the wise Bible scholar that he is, pointed out the rest of the Scripture to Katie and me. This particular night, Katie was in increased pain and had been crying most of the day, so he read out the complete passage of Philippians 4:11-13.

> *...for I have learned how to be content with whatever I have. I know how to live on almost nothing or with everything. I have learned the secret of living in every situation, whether it is with a full stomach or empty, with*

plenty or little. For I can do everything through Christ, who gives me strength.

My husband pointed out to me that the verse we Christians always quote and speak out like some sort of victory chant and mantra is actually *not* about just being able to do anything and everything with Christ at your side—it's about the struggle. It's about making it through the struggle and the trial.

It's about Jesus, not me.

Whatever the circumstance, no matter how difficult, I can have confidence in the fact that He will not leave me to make it through on my own. Honestly, I don't think I could make it on my own at all. I *know* I can't. Without the hope of Jesus, without the strength He provided and continues to provide through these times, I would be lost in this.

This contentment comes only through Jesus. I am unable to be content on my own. But when I refocus my attention onto the One who holds in His hands every moment we are facing, then I can rest. I can be satisfied. I'm still not sure about the "happy," but satisfaction and rest will suffice.

Throughout those years, there were brief moments when I felt content. But five minutes later, I was once more out of my mind with worry and anxiety. It was a vicious cycle. When life gets hard, the contentment gets hard. When you know the character of God, it makes being content in the "whatever" easier. Our circumstances don't change anything about Him. When our life is good, He is good. When our life sucks, He is good. And, in either scenario, He is in control. I am still learning to be content in that.

IT WOULD END THIS WAY
Richard

I have fought the good fight; I have finished the race; I have kept the faith.
- 2 Timothy 4:7 (NIV)

November 11, 2016.

It was a day of immense rejoicing, tempered by the knowledge that Katie's road to recovery was far from over. After ten months and six days of complete hospital hell, Katie was released from Texas Children's Hospital (TCH), and thus began yet another roller coaster of emotions, trials, and high points. Our champion princess was showing, yet again, that she was extremely strong, resilient, and determined to get better.

She fought daily to walk again. Although she needed help and much more therapy, Katie went from not being able to sit up on her own to walking from room to room in our apartment. She went from needing adult diapers to using a bedside commode to going to the bathroom on her own. She went from having to get wipe-downs in her bed to being able to take a bath with just our assistance getting her in and out of the tub. She was making great strides.

Despite all her progress, we still spent most of our time back at TCH. Our typical time out of the hospital was about a week. Then she would get put back in, usually due to some kind of fever or infection. Katie would do anything in her power not to have to be put back inpatient, even telling her doctor she would just use oral Morphine to cope with one of her painful bouts of pancreatitis. This girl wanted to be home with her parents and her puppy, Roxy. She wanted to feel as normal as she could, despite how much pain she was in.

In 2016, we spent every holiday inpatient. In 2017, we were inpatient for every holiday through July. However, she got discharged on Father's Day. Daphne and I made plans to just go home with our girl, but Katie insisted on going to dinner at a restaurant for this special occasion. We're so glad she forced our hand on that one. Katie was always about quality time, no matter what.

She continued to struggle with her health issues while also continuing to get stronger. We just knew our amazing girl would be the one who made it through this, for she had already made it through more than most.

Between her intermittent hospital stays, Katie started homebound school again. She was completing the assignments at a great pace and her teachers were pleased with her progress. She was set to catch up and become a full-fledged junior for Fall 2017! Our days were still busy at TCH, even when we weren't inpatient. We settled into a schedule of dialysis three days a week for four hours each day, and dropped to one or two BMT clinic visits each week. As I once told Daphne, "We have mastered the art of taking care of a sick child." We had it down—schedule, meds, hospital visits, leisure time, eating out—all of it.

Two new problems arose for Katie over those last months: hemolytic anemia (the body's destruction of its own red blood cells brought on by the many blood transfusions she received over the years) and COP (cryptogenic organizing pneumonia—a particularly stubborn form of pneumonia). Both of these were typically treated with steroids. However, due to Katie's history of steroid use and the effects of the long-term doses, this was not a good option for her; she was being treated with an alternative medicine for the hemolytic anemia, but with the new diagnosis of COP, there was no other option. Katie was starting to require oxygen on a daily basis, and this type of pneumonia would only disappear with steroids. After consulting multiple doctors, the decision was made to tailor this treatment to Katie's specific needs, closely watching for any signs of change. Her primary doctor was always concerned about Katie going back on steroids, as were we, but there were no other options. We would just have to try. After a month into the treatment, Katie seemed to be doing well.

The week before Katie was scheduled for another round of steroids and her typical clinic/dialysis visit, she begged us to have a family night. Not just a family night at home, but a night out. So of course, we did. Daphne had just gone back to working full-time, so I packed up Katie's stuff (at this point, I was a pro at packing stuff and getting all of her things ready), and she and I headed to the aquarium in downtown Houston. Daphne would meet us there after work.

Katie and I got there before Daphne, so we went through about half of the exhibits without her, then repeated the process once Daphne got there. It didn't bother Katie at all to see all those fish a second time (she loved watching fish). She was just happy to be out doing *something*. We ate dinner at the aquarium's restaurant, though of course, Katie only ate a few bites of soup and bread; she was anxious to play games and ride the Ferris wheel. She had brought all her quarters to play, but ended up not needing them because the attendants just kept giving her many more chances than the average person. We joked about how being in the wheelchair was to her advantage for this kind of stuff. Daphne and I helped her navigate getting from the wheelchair onto the train and the Ferris wheel. It was a big night, and it completely exhausted her. As we think back on that night, we're so grateful for that time together, because it would prove to be our last family outing.

The next morning, we went to Katie's regular Friday clinic/dialysis visit. She complained about back pain but was still in good spirits. The pain was, most likely, due to the fact that she spent the entire night before in her wheelchair, so we didn't give it much thought. But another more serious issue still lurked: she needed a blood transfusion, which had become pretty normal since the hemolytic anemia had resurfaced. We all continued to have faith that she would overcome all of this. She had already overcome so much. This hemolytic anemia thing was just another kink in the plan.

Even with that little kink, from a clinical point of view, she was doing well. Her doctor even told me that, if we wanted to, we could go home (as in Lafayette) for a day or two, with the understanding that, should she need attention, we were to immediately make the three-and-a-half-hour drive to report back to the hospital. It was a concession we were more than willing to make. Katie hadn't been back "home" for almost two years. It's what she looked forward to the most. We were looking forward to that trip too, so very much. She longed to see her friends in Lafayette, and the doctor's words gave us great hope that she was finally, truly, on the mend. Katie had already worked out a guest list for her seventeenth birthday party, which was to occur in our hometown within about two months!

However, by Sunday, Katie wasn't feeling well. I was working that day and Daphne was with her at the apartment. She collapsed on the floor, unconscious, only to wake up vomiting. Just as Daphne was about to call an ambulance, Katie became more lucid and begged her not to. She said she felt better and was going to see the doctor in the morning anyway. ER visits were pretty traumatic for our girl, and she had seen many of them over the year, so Daphne called me to come home early and help get her up. The rest of the day, Katie just seemed tired, so we put her to bed early, knowing she had to be up for that clinic visit. At about 2:00 am, she woke up vomiting again, and we debated about bringing her in. But again, this wasn't anything out of the ordinary, unfortunately.

I brought Katie in for her visit that Monday morning. Her hemoglobin was very low—this explained the weakness—so blood was ordered. She also required oxygen again, which meant we were headed for another readmission.

After several units of blood and desperate pleas not to go through the ER (the BMT clinic cannot authorize transfers straight to PICU), we made our way down to the ER, where we went through the regular course of action (stress doses of *everything*, and lots of ado over, usually, nothing) before we got moved to PICU.

It was an old familiar room, one we'd been in before. It had been a while since we'd seen the PICU, and it became more like a reunion with some of our favorite doctors and nurses. We all figured this would be another short visit.

Everything was going as normal, except for the decision to include an extra dose of steroids to, hopefully, stave off the hemolysis and help with the pneumonia. Things were looking up, and by Wednesday, we were just waiting for a room to become available on the bone marrow floor.

But things changed on Thursday.

I left the room to go for a walk (walks around the hospital were often necessary to retain my sanity) and, within fifteen minutes, my phone rang. The nurse on the other end of the line told me that Katie had fallen and wanted me back with her.

When I got back to the PICU front desk, I was told I couldn't go back, because one of the patients was coding. I quickly explained that I had gotten a phone call to come back, and when I told her who I was, the front desk person gave me a serious look and immediately let me back into the unit. That frightened me a little.

My fears met with reality as I got back to Katie's room and found it full of doctors and nurses, with blood everywhere. Katie had not only fallen while trying to go to the bedside commode, but she also had another large GI bleed.

This had not happened in a year.

Katie was nervous and a little shaken, but calm. Not wanting to say anything in front of her, I texted Daphne to come in. My logic was of no use, though, because, as one would imagine, that text resulted in a panicked return phone call. Daphne immediately left work early and headed to meet us in PICU.

At this point, we began to relive all of the horrors of the previous year. Katie was intubated, sedated, and pumped with several units of blood. Once she was stabilized, we began discussing the cause of the bleeding and how to find it. A couple of hours later, we went down for an upper GI scope, which revealed no sign of actual bleeding, just general oozing. We were encouraged to find no signs of direct bleeding, but we also knew this drill and knew it wasn't over just yet.

Two days later, it happened again.

On her way down for another scope (lower GI, this time), while in transport, she began to bleed. This development stunned us all, and we began to wonder

180

why this would start happening again. All signs pointed to the stress doses of steroids, but no one could discover a clear answer. Again, the scope yielded no well-defined results as we spent the next two weeks watching Katie get weaker and weaker.

Her body overloaded with more fluids. The hemolysis increased. The fevers rampaged. Her oxygen saturations dropped lower than normal and her breathing became more labored.

Even after several tests, there was still no sign of what was causing the infection and fever. Her blood pressure kept falling and her breathing became ever shallower, and we just knew this time was different. Things just weren't getting better. Our dreams of taking our sweet girl back to our hometown were fading.

On Saturday, July 15th, she was intubated for the last time. The PICU team increased her pain meds, and started her on a paralytic so the ventilator could take over her breathing.

We were devastated. On Sunday, we booked a flight for Kylie to return from Australia. Daphne's parents began to make their way from Southeast Asia. Houston pastors and friends came to see us and pray with us. Lafayette friends made plans to visit her one last time. We began to have those conversations we never wanted or even imagined, realizing that our baby girl would soon leave us for her eternal reward.

THAT GIRL
Richard

If ever there is a tomorrow when we're not together,
there is something you must always remember. You are
braver than you believe, stronger than you seem, and
smarter than you think. But the most important thing is
even if we are apart, I'll always be with you.
-A.A. Milne, *The Pooh Storybook*

One person we haven't really written about yet is Katie's older sister, Kylie. Throughout Katie's journey, Daphne and I have had more than our fair share of guilt for not being able to spend enough time with her. Of course, Kylie understands, but that doesn't make the feelings of regret go away.

When everything started with Katie, we were one month away from Kylie's high school graduation and all that goes with that milestone event: senior prom dress-shopping, graduation photo shoots, last-minute wisdom-imparting conversations, and just time spent with our ever-adult-becoming, once-wispy-haired-and-overall-wearing, *Little-Mermaid*-watching princess.

My wife once put it this way: this was supposed to be her time.

It was supposed to be her time to be celebrated, to be reflected upon, to be (grudgingly) eased out of the nest and into full-fledged adulthood. It was supposed to be all about her—except that it became all about her little sister.

Instead of looking to Kylie for those celebration events, we looked to her for a stem cell match. We looked to her to take care of the house in our absence during Katie's transplant days. And before we knew it, we were looking on as she boarded a plane and headed to Australia for ministry school.

One of the many fascinating things about raising siblings is seeing their differences and similarities magnified, sometimes on an hourly basis. While Katie was over-the-top flamboyant, Kylie was more reserved. Kylie loved random nonsense humor while Katie was a supreme pun-mistress. Kylie was our musical prodigy while Katie was our soccer star. But they both shared a deep love for Jesus, the desire to influence their friends for Him, and a commitment to our family, for which I will be eternally grateful.

Our girls were truly a blast to be with, twenty-four-seven.

People have been quick to label Katie as the crazy one, but I've watched Kylie win a dance contest at one of her mother's women's events. I'm not sure what you would *call* her kind of dancing, but the crowd loved it, and the more they cheered, the bigger the dance became. I've seen her have fun in any situation, from eating out with me to revealing complete craziness on social media. She loves being herself, and I've loved watching her discover who that self is.

She's her own fashion icon. Her hair has been every color under the sun, and she's even experimented with corn-row weaves and dreadlocks. No perm needed for her once-wisps—she has the full-on curly curls, although the humidity in both southwest Louisiana and Sydney, Australia love wreaking havoc on them. She goes from eighties dorkiness to hipster in two seconds flat. From city girl dressed to the nines to tomboy on the back forty, she runs the gamut of clothing choice, yet it all seems to work for her.

And let's not forget her musical talents. This girl started out on piano, but ventured out to several other instruments. Guitar, bass, ukulele, and accordion, plus a few others added in along the way. When she was around five years old, we were told she might actually have perfect pitch, and she's only blossomed from there. She won a statewide competition in songwriting, progressing to the national level. She was the first non-senior to make it into the advanced music class at her high school, paving the way for other underclassmen to enter that ensemble. And I haven't even started on her incredible singing voice. Seriously, as a musician, Kylie is the real deal in every single way. And I'm not just saying that as a doting dad (though maybe a little)—I'm saying it as a degreed musician who can hear the difference.

Kylie has always been a thinker. Even at a young age, we noticed she processed things a little differently. With the exception of a couple of teen years, she's had a love for books and reading, which, thankfully, has followed her into adult life. She loves books about psychology, science, and the like, but her passion for reading and studying has become fixated upon correct theological methodology, and how to really apply Scripture to a life situation.

Perhaps that all started because of her Christian school upbringing. Perhaps she just grew up in a ministry home, hanging around with college-aged ministry students. Perhaps God has been speaking things to her since Day One. Perhaps she is much smarter than she lets on, in many ways.

While in a parent-teacher conference, Kylie's sixth-grade teacher shared with us a story about a classroom question-and-answer time. As Kylie raised her hand to ask a question, the following scenario unfolded:

187

"Mrs. Richardson, you know how, in the Bible, when an Israelite was in mourning, he or she would rend their garment, then put on sackcloth and ashes?

"Yes," came the reply.

"And, you know how, when Jesus died, the Bible says that the temple veil was torn in two?"

"Of course," said Mrs. Richardson, not totally sure where things were headed.

"Well, we've always been told that the veil tearing was God opening up the holy of holies, so that we could all gain access to the presence of God."

"Yes."

"Could it be, that, the veil was torn in two, from top to bottom, because God was grieving over the death of His Son, Jesus?"

A more beautiful and complicated question, revealing a more inquisitive person, I have not ever heard or seen, even in my year of Bible college and subsequent years around Bible students and teachers. This child seemed to have found a hidden gem of God's character.

Kylie has also, like her youngest sister, shown herself to be completely fearless. At eighteen years old, she left America to pursue a ministry and music dream. More on that situation later, but, during a phone conversation, she revealed to me that she had just bought a cello.

Knowing her Australian financial situation, and how there was no way she could afford something like that, my hover-dad instincts kicked in. "How did you get the money to buy one?"

"Well, a friend of mine spotted me the money to get it. It was only a hundred and fifty bucks. I'm doing a gig with it, so when I get paid for it, I'll pay her back."

I was a little stunned. As a string major myself, who struggled for at least a year to get a barely decent

188

(and in-tune) sound out of a bowed upright bass, I couldn't believe the audacity and bravery to book a gig before even learning an instrument like that. "But Kylie, you don't play cello!"

"I do now."

I'm still a little amazed at her daring in that situation. When I asked her later how the gig went, she said, "Fine," like it was no big deal. I would *never* have done something like that. Even to this day, I still struggle with bowing technique and pitch, but those things didn't seem to bother her.

And now, back to the America-leaving, and the Australia-conquering…

Kylie has always had a ministry-minded slant. She knew, from an early age, that she wanted to go to a ministry school. For a long time, she talked about going to our home church's leadership college, but based on the counsel of two of the program's staff members, the main leader and the music instructor, she decided instead to look at other options. She simply had more music training than she would have gotten there, and both of them told her their program really had nothing to offer her outside of discipleship training. Truth be known, it was God's doing all along, because halfway through what would have been her first year there, the music instructor, who is also her godmother, moved to Boston with her husband and family to begin the process of planting a church there.

As Kylie began to look at other programs, her mother and I made suggestions here and there, but when Daphne mentioned that Hillsong had a program, she was instantly sold. Of course, I wanted her to stay in Lafayette with us, and my reasoning was perfectly far-sighted and logical (and safe).

"Kylie, you want to be a worship leader. Stay here and get a music degree. You're already leading worship in the church's youth ministry and main auditorium, and I'm sure Eric (the campus pastor at our local university) would have you leading worship for him. If I were a pastor and your resume came across my desk, having led worship at three different places, one being the main auditorium of a megachurch, with an actual music degree, you're the first person I'm calling."

Her reply still rings in my head, signifying the war was over before it started. "But... Australia, Dad."

It was a foregone conclusion. A fight that could never be won. My baby girl was moving to the Land Down Under and there was nothing I could do to stop it.

But a couple of conversations really put things into perspective for me. The first came when discussing the situation with one of my coworkers, a wise counselor whose opinions I've always trusted. He said something that just really made sense.

"I'd rather have my daughter halfway around the world, going after God with her whole heart, than in my backyard backslidden or just sitting on a pew."

The other conversation was one I only heard about. Our pastor and a dear friend of mine were discussing how their daughters, who are roughly the same age, were both leaving the country for a season. One was traveling to Africa to work at an orphanage; the other was going to Australia to study at Youth With a Mission. Obviously, both men were gravely concerned about seeing their respective baby girls head off to other continents, but my friend's observation was priceless in its wisdom:

"We've prayed every day since before they were born for God to make them world-changers. Now that He's doing it, we can't go back on our prayers."

Both of these conversations brought great peace, although that peace became tempered as Katie's situation began to develop. At first, we thought Katie

190

would get her transplant, we'd be home, she'd get better, Kylie would leave, and we'd go on like normal. I viewed Kylie's nest-leaving as a normal progression, although I hated to have to do it, nonetheless.

But things became not-normal on Tuesday, January 5th, 2016, when Daphne took Katie back to Houston for an admission that would last over ten months, followed by another eight months of in-and-out hospital stays and Katie's ultimate passing.

My plan was to leave that Friday to be with Daphne and Katie. Kylie came by my office on Wednesday or Thursday and we had a serious conversation about Katie and where we were headed as a family. The graft versus host diagnosis was not on the table as of yet; all we knew was that Katie was really ill, that it would be a while before we had a definitive answer, and that answer could prove to be scarier than any of the unknowns.

As I began explaining the situation, I could see great concern in Kylie's expression. She was becoming torn between the desires for her life and the desires to be with Katie during her most trying time. Her question to me in that moment told me of the weight she bore in her mind and heart.

"Daddy, is all of this happening because I'm not supposed to go to Hillsong?"

My heart sank. No eighteen-year-old girl should have to wrestle with the emotions that come with seeing her baby sister wrestling with what no fourteen-year-old should have to face.

"Absolutely not," I said. "One doesn't have anything to do with the other." I was trying my best to be a source of peace for her, guiding her to make the most informed decision she could in that moment. "God doesn't work that way. He would never punish Katie for something you're doing."

"But it will be hard on you guys if I go."

"Kylie, I look at it this way: you're eighteen, almost nineteen. You're an adult now. If you were twenty-eight, living your own life, and your underage sibling had an issue, I would never dream of asking you to stop your life to come help us. Your mother and I got this. You need to pursue your dreams. If anything, this is an attack of the enemy to keep your mind from focusing on what God has called you to."

I could see that this was bringing her some sense of relief, so I decided to tell her a story I'd heard. "Do you know who Arnold Schwarzenegger is?"

She nodded her head in the affirmative.

"Well, when he first competed for Mr. Olympia, his dad had just died. As a matter of fact, he missed his dad's funeral. His family was furious with him, but he said that it's what he and his dad had dreamed of for years, and nothing was going to bring his dad back. He won that year, and won several times afterward. What if he had listened to his family? We might not ever know who he is today."

(After researching that story for this book, what I found was that this story never happened. Apparently, Arnold's dad was quite abusive, and he chose not to go because of that. The whole storyline was fabricated, and added into the plot of Arnold's first movie, *Pumping Iron*, because the producers thought it was more interesting than the actual facts. Upon sharing my *faux pas* with Kylie, she joked about her whole life being a lie, but that she got the point. So much for my great parable-telling…)

I then reiterated to her the need to follow her dreams. I told her that I loved the fact that she dreamed big and that we believed God had great things in store for her.

Three weeks later, I watched her walk through the security gate at Bush Intercontinental Airport in Houston. I was so proud of her in that moment, but my daddy heart was completely crushed. Both of my daughters were facing unknowns of their own. Daphne and I were also way out in completely uncharted waters. But I was still proud of both of them, nonetheless.

Living in Australia with a sibling facing such a tenuous situation in America wasn't the easiest thing for Kylie. Her sleep patterns were off. She told me of many times where she felt disconnected, but not in the way it would normally present itself. Instead of emotional disconnection, she felt guilt and sadness that she just couldn't be there with us. She, like the rest of us, had to trust that God was working for our collective good.

And He was.

One day, in one of her classes, she got a wonderful confirmation. Her teacher, one of Hillsong's pastors, was pacing the front of the room while going through the curriculum, and he stopped right in front of her. He looked at her and said, "God wants you to know that, whatever is happening back home, He's got that under control, and you're right where you need to be. Does that mean anything to you?"

Of course it did! She knew where she was supposed to be, and when she shared that story with me, it brought great peace to me, as well. My baby girl heard the voice of God as to where she should go and it was confirmed though others. It made me proud she had decided on that school at that season of her life, despite my best intentions for a "safe" plan.

After Katie's passing, we went to Lafayette for the funeral and then headed back to Houston to go through Katie's things, get Kylie sent off to Australia again, and pack to move back to Louisiana. On Kylie's last day in the States, I took her out on a little date night (steak with Dad had become the date *du jour* since her early teen years). We went to a great place in Houston, and she actually cried a little when she bit into her filet mignon, saying it was the best steak she ever had. On the ride home, we began to talk about that day when I counseled her to make the move. I asked her the same question I posed to Daphne on the day Katie passed away.

"Do you have any regrets?"

She said she did, but they mostly centered around the fact that she was so far away, so I posed another question: "If you had not gone and had come here with us, would you have the desire to do anything in ministry now?"

She said that she would probably just have a job and would have settled into a life of just working, but that she has grown so much since she left, and that she could see how God had taken her into such new levels of relationships, learning, musicality, and walking with Him. I told her I would never want her just to settle for anything, and that her answer confirmed why I told her to go.

But I also told her how difficult it was.

I told her it was heart-wrenching. I told her how I sat in the car, crying for at least fifteen minutes, after she got on that plane the first time. I told her it doesn't get much easier, seeing her leave each time. But the last thing I said, through tears, really seemed to make a lot of sense to her.

"Kylie, I'm not sure where it is in the Bible, but there is a verse that says 'hope deferred makes the heart sick.' I already had a child who was sick in her body. I couldn't have another child who was sick in her heart." I also told her it was a calculated risk on my behalf, but one I gladly took, to see her grow into all she could be, and not wait any longer to see it happen. She thanked

194

me for making those tough choices, which meant the world to me.

I'm so thankful to be her daddy. I'm so thankful that I get to see her grow, travel, learn, and have her world enlarged so much more than she could have ever imagined. Maybe Daphne was right all along. This was supposed to be her time, just not in the way we had originally thought.

DON'T CALL US "INSPIRING"
Richard and Daphne

*Let your roots grow down into Him, and let your lives be built on
Him. Then your faith will grow strong in the truth you were
taught, and you will overflow with thankfulness.*
- Colossians 2:7 (NLT)

"Inspiring."

That's the word we heard a lot. On an almost-daily basis, actually. We grew to hate that word.

We didn't feel inspiring. We never set out to be. We simply wanted to do what was right by our child. When did just doing the right thing mean that you're an inspiration? Isn't that the bare minimum that should be done in any situation?

Sometimes, life just leaves you no choice. It forces you to make decisions you never thought you'd have to make. That's what happened with us. We knew our steps were ordered by God, but that didn't make it any easier. Although we trusted God, this was still very hard.

We had to make many difficult decisions: move away from our friends and family, resign our positions, and put ourselves in a place where we had to completely trust God in every area of our lives and our marriage. There were lots of tears. But we knew what we had to do for our family and that God had lined it all out for us.

We always thought marriage was pretty easy. Really, for us it has been. Most of the time. Of course, we've had rough patches throughout our two-plus decades together, but nothing compared to what we had to deal with during Katie's illness.

Never in a million years did we imagine we would have to walk through this nightmare. That's when we learned we had to lean on each other the most. We became all each other had. When one of us was falling apart, the other would be strong and comforting. We'd take turns playing these roles until Katie's passing. To be honest, we are still playing those roles.

When we made our marriage vows, we pledged to stay together in sickness and in health, for richer or poorer, until death parted us. The day we made those vows, we were okay with assuming the sickness in question would happen to either of us; we had no idea it would present itself in one of our daughters.

When life is gut-wrenchingly painful, emotions run high. Everything we dealt with internally affected what happened on the outside. Things were said. We hurt each other's feelings. We also didn't get much time to spend together like we used to... the date nights, the boring nights on the couch watching TV, cooking together in the kitchen, alone time, and you know... the intimate stuff married people need to do. Yeah, all that stuff became last on the list.

This contributed to the pain, the hurt, the heartbreak. The next thing we knew, we were in arguments over the most inconsequential things. Add exhaustion to the mix and we could not have been on shakier ground. But we tried our best to take as much time alone as humanly possible. Unfortunately, it was ridiculously hard.

So we tried to adjust. We took moments. A walk to Subway for a sandwich while Katie slept became our version of a date.

Looking back on the situation, we never really set out to have a formal plan on how we dealt with the ups and downs, but, thankfully, everything fell into place. We realized, in the heat of those moments, that we were learning to lean on each other, that we saw ourselves as a team, and that we needed to focus on "us."

And we tried to not "lose ourselves," which was the advice given to us by one of our many nurse-friends. It was hard to do, because when you have a child who is battling sickness and fighting for her life, nothing else matters. Your own identity gets put on the back burner and being a protector and advocate for your child comes to the forefront. You simply become "Mom" and "Dad." In fact, that's the name everyone in the hospital uses for you. The staff doesn't call you by your name... only "Mom" or "Dad." Those were our identities.

In these times, you don't even remember who you were, much less know who you *are* anymore. You don't remember what dreams you had. You don't remember even what future you had hoped for. You don't know who you are nor care about that. You only care about being that mom or dad your child needs.

One of Daphne's journal entries made this confession about her identity:

My identity has become pretty simple:
I am a child of God.
I am a wife.
I am a mom.

That's literally it.
There are no other titles I hold anymore.

Those are the only titles I have to work on every day and the only ones that matter.
There was a time when I did have goals and dreams for myself, but those have faded away.
There were times when I agonized about God's calling on my life and whether I was doing what I was supposed to be doing, doing the right thing. Now, there is no doubt.
This is my calling. This is my life.
I don't know what the future holds for me. I don't know what the future holds for my family.
I only know Who holds the future, and I trust Him.

Every day, I am learning to embrace the ministry that God has put in front of me. I am trying desperately to be content in a circumstance I would wish on no one.

When I lose myself, I just have to remember that God knows who I am. He knows EXACTLY who I am, actually better than I do. My identity is only found in who I am through my relationship with Him.

As a parent, when something catastrophic happens to your child, a natural instinct rises up to protect. We even had shirts that said, "Papa Bear," "Mama Bear," and "Baby Bear." That's what parents do. They protect their cubs. But when there's nothing you can do to protect your cub, the pain you experience is agonizing.

And that's where we found ourselves.

As we've tried to describe in other chapters, Katie's pain was extreme, for long periods of time, with little to no relief. So was our pain for her. We felt helpless.

One month after Katie's admission for graft versus host, Daphne wrote the following:

It's hard to tell the difference between day and night here.

The blinds stay shut.

The lights stay off.

I sit in silence.

No voices.

No noise.

Just silence.

Day in, day out.

My girl wants it that way.

It helps her cope with the pain.

I quietly sit next to her bed.

Watching her.

Praying.

My heart ripping.

Aching.

Broken.

Wanting answers.

Expecting good news for this day.

Crying.

Waiting.

Tired.

Exhausted.

I sit longing for the day that light will break through this darkness.

The day when I can pull the shade up.

The day when she feels like her old self.

The day she sits up from her bed, looks at me, and smiles.

The day she laughs again.

It's been a long time.

My heart yearns for that day.

I'm ready for a breakthrough.

I sit in darkness today.

Waiting for the light promised in tomorrow.

I thank God today for His light that is always present even in our darkest hours. It's there even when we cannot see it.... when the darkness is overwhelming. Some days look pretty bleak. It seems like the darkness will never end. But, then the dawn appears. It ALWAYS appears. It has to. There won't be darkness forever.

Another way we tried to protect Katie was to constantly remind her of her worth. At one point, she described herself as "ugly." It was heartbreaking to hear, because all we saw was beauty and strength when we looked at her.

She was chosen to carry the torch for the hospital's celebration of the opening ceremony of the 2016 Summer Olympics. When she asked, "Why me?" the answer was "because you're a champion." There was *no doubt* that she was a true champion, and totally deserved to carry that torch.

We had to sign a release form so that TCH could photograph her. We asked Katie if she was okay with that. She said she was.

We didn't post many pictures of Katie because she didn't look like her old self. The steroids really damaged her body... major damage to her skin and, of course, the "moon face."

She decided to fix her hair and even put on makeup for the ceremony. When she looked in the mirror, she said she was ugly.... that her face was fat, her hair was thin and didn't look good, her skin was covered in stretch marks and bruises, and so on and so forth.

If she only knew how beautiful she really was.

After Daphne told her that she was definitely not ugly, but beautiful, she said, "Mama, I see the way people look at me."

That broke our hearts even more. But we knew it was true, because we saw the way people looked at her. They didn't mean any harm, but when they looked at her, they saw a sick child. We hated that because she was so much more.

Richard told her, "People are shallow. They don't think about what others have been through. I promise you that anyone who sees you and knows your story will see only a beautiful young woman who has

205

faced things in her life that no one should have to face. And you conquered it. And one day, you'll meet a man, and although you may hate your scars, he will love and cherish them, because they will have given him the best gift of his life: you."

She never met that "man" here on earth. But the One she's with now adores her, scars and all.

Another statement we heard a lot was, "I don't know how you do it."

Our life was not easy. It was actually the hardest it had ever been. Those years were ruthless.

Five months into Katie's ten-month hospital stay, Daphne wrote this:

I still have to remind myself daily that this is real. Our lives have changed. And, changed drastically.

I walk outside and immediately think of how much Katie would enjoy the sunshine, fresh air, birds chirping, and the smell of freshly cut grass.

When I wake each morning, I think about how I'd love to hop up and cook some breakfast for her and plan what we could do for the day.

I look at all the social media posts about her friends getting their driver's licenses, going to dances, and attending summer camps, and it makes me sad that she's not getting to do those things.

These are the kinds of thoughts that run through a mama's head on a daily basis when her child is fighting for her life in a hospital bed for what seems like an eternity.

I still cry. A lot.

I wish it wasn't so. I wish I could be much stronger. I will never get used to this kind of life we're living. I will never get used to seeing my daughter hurting. Never.

As Richard said last night, while I was crying yet again, "You're just a mama."

So true. I'm just a mama who wants her child healthy, not hurting, enjoying a normal life.

That's all.

I try to be positive. I ask the doctors for the "best case scenario." I find things to be thankful for each day. I encourage my daughter to do the same.

But this doesn't get any easier. Time doesn't help. It makes it worse. It makes it harder.

Don't get me wrong. I still trust God. I still believe He's here with us. He's not forsaken us. He's holding us through all the hurting and all the pain. Why His plan doesn't look like the good plan I have in my head, I'll never know. But I have no other choice than to trust a loving Father, who is always faithful and always good.

But it doesn't make things hurt any less. It doesn't make me less exhausted. It just gives me hope that there is something better and beautiful coming, no matter how impatiently I wait for it.

We know *how* we did it. It was only Jesus. It was only God's grace that carried us. It didn't always feel that way, though. Sometimes, it felt like we were drowning, with nothing and no one to grab onto. But, the water always subsided, most of the time, simply to rise again another day.

We had to come to grips with the fact that it may have been something we would have to deal with the rest of our lives. Things might have gotten better. Things might have become more manageable. Our job was to just handle it the best we could.

Some days, the second half of Ephesians 6:13 and the beginning of the next verse were all we had to cling to.

"Having done all, to stand. Stand therefore,"

That's how we "did it."

Whatever is thrown at you, you just have to deal with it. There's no escape, no running and hiding, no letting someone else handle it for you. You have to deal with the trials of life and unforeseen circumstances.

Life is tough. There's just no way around it. Trials will come. Jesus promised it. He said, "Here on earth you *will* have many trials and sorrows…" (John 16:33, NLT) And just because you feel ready to take them head on, that doesn't mean you'll actually be able to do that.

We thought we were mentally and spiritually prepared for anything. We had all the knowledge of what we needed to do, needed to feel, needed to believe, and needed to pray for. But none of that stopped the doubt and questions that arose, and we're disappointed in how we both completely fell apart many times.

We thought we were stronger. As it turns out, we weren't.

But that didn't stop us from giving it our best. No matter how tough things got, we were determined to do what we had to do. We could cry about it as much as we wanted, but it didn't change what we knew we had to do.

We didn't know when we'd all get th
if or when it would be over, but we did kno\
end of that same verse, John 16:33, there is
on earth you will have many trials and sorro
heart, because I have overcome the world."

Jesus overcame, which means we could
overcome. And yes... one day it would be "over." It just
wouldn't be the way we wanted it.

Another lesson we learned in this process was
not to sweat the small stuff. Through this, our
perspectives changed, and we decided to not waste brain
power on things that just don't matter in the grand
scheme of life.

Sometimes, our gratefulness is associated with
singular events or occurrences in our lives. But
gratefulness is a way of living. Living a grateful life is
nurturing a heart of constant gratitude, not only in good
times, but also in bad. That's not an easy thing to do in
hard times, but that's when you find out what you're truly
made of. When you have a grateful heart, you can
remain grateful even when you are lacking, when your
need hasn't been met, and when you have no answers.

One thing we wish we could say a million times
over is this: take time throughout your day to notice all
you have and all you have had in this life. Be grateful for
it. Be grateful for the breath you get to breathe when you
wake in the morning. Be grateful for the simple things,
like packing school lunches, shopping for groceries,
holding the hands of your little ones and your spouse,
and sharing a home with the ones you love.

We realized we weren't grateful enough. What
we would give today to be picking up dirty clothes off
the floor or mediating an argument between sisters.

In the midst of trying times, we have to
purposefully make our hearts grateful. We should

intentionally look for things throughout the day for which to be grateful.

We thank God for the blessings He granted us through the journey and we also thank Him for the restoration He promises to bring. We thank God for so many precious, tender moments we got to experience with Katie that truly showed us her heart. We thank God for the dreams He's allowing our oldest daughter to live out. We thank God for the provision He granted us and for the provision still to come. We thank God that knowing Him allows us always to be able to say, "Everything will be okay."

Even in the midst of people telling us how we were "rockstar parents," there were plenty of mistakes being made. Tempers still flared. We still hurt each other and, sadly, hurt Katie. In May of 2017, Richard had a humbling experience with Katie, detailed below:

> So, a few things have changed in our world. Daphne is now working, and I am now Mr. Mom-ing it for the next few months or so. I'm trying to do some consulting things here and there, to be a blessing to smaller churches who can't afford a full-time media guy, plus playing a few jazz gigs and worship services as they come along, but mainly, I'm Katie's main caregiver.
>
> This has its share of challenges for me.
>
> I'm used to being the "fun" one.
>
> I'm used to being the one the girls can look at and roll their eyes when Daphne turns all "Helicopter Mom." I'm used to being the one who earns the paycheck and controls the finances. I'm used to being in charge.

Even though we've been inpatient for almost all of 2016, and then over seventy-five percent of 2017, I'm still used to being out in the world and not in the hospital. I don't EVER want to get used to the hospital life. Never, ever. Never. Ever.

With all that said, this particular hospital stay has been especially tiresome and straining. I don't have a job to go to. I don't have other people to talk to. I don't have my wife here with me, to take turns throughout the day. It's all me, and it's exhausting. And I know me, and I know when I'm reaching my limits with things, and I know that, although I can't predict with relative certainty how I will react, I KNOW that I WILL react.

Tomorrow, three friends of mine are coming to visit me. They're bringing handguns. We're gonna go shooting and then consume large quantities of meat. I think I just grew a little more chest hair as I typed that statement (although, in full disclosure, the statement, as was the rest of this post, was typed on Katie's MacBook Air with a floral-pattern protective case). It was from a comment in a text conversation with one of the guys coming that I got the idea to write this post. He wrote this:

"You set the tone when it comes to being a man. The true definition of manning up!!! You inspire others!"

Instantly, upon reading that text, tears filled my eyes (as they are now, even as I type this out on the aforementioned girly laptop). People see me way differently than I see myself, and they don't know what goes on in my head and heart, 24/7.

Here's a prime example of my wonderful, bar-setting, inspiration-inspiring dad moments:

Yesterday, the physical and occupational therapists came over to do some work with Katie. To say that she hates doing PT/OT is as much of an understatement as calling Drew Brees a "good" quarterback. And it's the same old story with her, almost every time. She doesn't feel good, she's tired, she's nauseous, blah, blah, blah. Granted, she does have a lot of pain and nausea, but sometimes I can't tell what is real and what is fabricated because of teenage drama (and Katie has never been short on the drama). At that point, I pretty much had enough. When she asked for ice to take an anti-nausea pill, our nurse offered to get it, but I jumped up and said, "No. Let me do it, because only 'daddy' can do those things." (A little backstory here. There have been NUMEROUS occasions where she was to get an injection or some other thing that nurses do, but she didn't want them to do it, but, rather, me. At first, it was endearing, but now it's become quite cumbersome.) Another reason I went to get it is because this particular nurse, although great, isn't exactly the fastest-moving person, and I wanted to get the PT/OT show on the road, knowing that the anti-nausea med would take some time to work. On my way out, I told Katie I wasn't putting up with her drama, and that she was gonna do what they wanted her to do, with no questions asked. I could instantly tell that I had embarrassed her.

But that didn't stop me.

When I returned to the room, I poured her tea over the ice and said, in the company of her nurse, and two PT/OT workers, "I have put my entire life on hold to see you regain your health, and yet you choose to continue to disrespect that by not doing what you should be doing." I gave her the pills and sat down. The PT/OT girls took

over, conducting their evaluation, then took her out a
*they did some walking (after much more balking on her
part).*

*Later that day, she quietly and humbly told me I
embarrassed her, and that I owed her an apology, and
before I could speak she also said that she owed me an
apology for not trying as hard as she should. We both
apologized, and that was it.*

Until I got the text.

*When I read it, I had this thought: I get frustrated with
my child, and I'm quick to remind her that we put
everything on hold for her (I've done it before). God did so
much more than that when He sent Jesus to be beaten,
spat upon, humiliated, cursed at, and ultimately, to die for
us, naked on a cross, and He never throws that in our
faces. He simply waits, mostly in silence, for us to come to
our senses, and repent.*

He is everything I'm not, and I'm nothing that He is.

1 Samuel 15:22-23 (NIV) says this:

*"But Samuel replied: 'Does the Lord delight in burnt
offerings and sacrifices as much as in obeying the Lord?
To obey is better than sacrifice, and to heed is better than
the fat of rams. For rebellion is like the sin of divination,
and arrogance like the evil of idolatry. Because you have
rejected the word of the Lord, he has rejected you as
king.'"*

*My "sacrifices" mean nothing, and my arrogance is
idolatry. And when it is all said and done, I do not want
to be rejected by God.*

213

God, help me to be the dad You want me to be. Help me to see that obedience in the position I hold, no matter how horrible, tiresome, or lowly, is better than any sacrifice I could ever make, for that position is my calling for that season of life. Help me to see that my worth is not in my income, status, or anything other than what You were willing to pay. Help me to see my worth in the eyes of my daughters. Help me to see my arrogance for what it is, and help me to run from it as I run to You.

You are truly everything I am not, but You are everything I aspire to be.

So, before you question how we did this, or tell us that we are "inspiring," just know that many times our humanness came to the forefront. But by inserting humility into the humanness, there was always forgiveness and acceptance.

And now, here we are, still as Katie's parents, with her no longer here. And honestly, things haven't changed for us all that much. The future remains uncertain to us. But our hope is in the fact that it's not uncertain to our God. We have to keep reminding ourselves that He sees us, He hears us, and He always has a plan for us that is for our good. We have to keep trusting in that fact.

All we can continue to do is hope and trust. When we got Katie's initial diagnosis, Daphne posted this statement: "'Against all hope... *in hope*, Abraham believed.' There is hope in hopeless situations."

The full Scripture Romans 4:18-22 (NLT), says this:

Even when there was no reason for hope, Abraham kept hoping—believing that he would become the father of many nations. For God had said to him, "That's how many descendants you will have!" And Abraham's faith did not weaken, even though, at about 100 years of age, he figured his body was as good as dead—and so was Sarah's womb. Abraham never wavered in believing God's promise. In fact, his faith grew stronger, and in this he brought glory to God. He was fully convinced that God is able to do whatever he promises. And because of Abraham's faith, God counted him as righteous.

We hoped. We trusted. We believed. We stood.

And still…

We hope. We trust. We believe. We stand.

ILEANA AND THE BLESSINGS
Richard

You can be sure that God will take care of everything you need, His generosity exceeding even yours in the glory that pours from Jesus.
- Philippians 4:19 (MSG)

No, that's not the name of a 1960s-era Russian British-Invasion-wannabe pop band.

In the roughly eighteen months leading up to Katie's initial diagnosis, our family was the beneficiary of some of the greatest financial blessings we had ever seen. It seemed like God was opening the literal doors of Heaven and pouring out blessings that we couldn't contain.

Let's recap so we can look at the bigger picture. From 2002 to 2016, I was the media director for a large church in Lafayette, Louisiana. For a couple of years, the department was just me, and then it grew to another person and me, and then it grew again to a total of four people. I hired Daphne as my production assistant/secretary, and she was with me for seven years. Shortly after taking that position, she was asked to take over the women's ministry at the church, which she did (on a volunteer basis) for nine years.

By 2012, our finances were really catching up to us, but not in a good way. Private college student loan repayment, a car and a house we probably couldn't afford, and no real budgeting on my part all came to a head that summer, when we found ourselves three months behind on our mortgage. It wasn't until mid-2013 until it was all sorted out, with a loan modification and some deferments, and things seemed to get back on track, though it was still a very tenuous situation. It started to affect me in all sorts of ways. I was constantly on edge about everything, and I just couldn't see my way out of the mess.

But in October of 2013, things began to change. Daphne was offered a position at a local real estate title company. We prayed about the change and decided to do it, because it would mean a little more financial freedom. Daphne accepted the position, which came with its share of positives and negatives. On the negative end, it was a much more rigid work environment (let's face it: I'm the coolest boss ever), and it took her away from one of her greatest passions: women's ministry. (Also, I lost an incredible employee, and I would often wonder if I had done the right thing, and if anyone could ever accuse me of a conflict-of-interest scenario.) On the positive end, Daphne would acquire a new skill, plus we would gain an extra five hundred dollars a month in our pockets. That may not seem like a lot, but for us, it was huge.

Most people, when presented with an increase in pay, think about how they can raise their standard of living. I was not concerned with this at all. I was more concerned about getting out of debt, doing wise things with our money, and being a blessing to others. We actually lowered our standard of living so we could put more money toward being truly free in our finances. With our newfound bump in income, the first thing we did was sell her car, which alleviated $368 in monthly payments. We made a small profit after paying it off, and paid cash for an older SUV. Thus began our debt snowball, and within one year, with only $6,000 of income, we paid off over $19,000 in credit card and medical bills! I can't even comprehend that math, outside of God's multiplication principles. Every time we paid off a bill, I'd post something on social media about it, always declaring God's faithfulness, always wanting to show others His goodness, always wanting to be a light to those who might have suffered faith-shaking trials.

There were many other blessings and opportunities that came our way after this. In January 2014, with one freelance video production job, I bought Kylie her first car. Affectionately known as "Linda," Kylie's red 2001 Volkswagen Beetle was the most fun I've ever had giving something away. It felt great to give her something she really wanted, and there were a few special "God moments" surrounding that situation that will be treasured memories for all of us. Later that year, I was able to purchase my own dream car with a long-term video job I scored. We were able to send missionaries to Romania. We were able to help families in need. We were finally able to see light at the end of the tunnel! We were able to fund, completely in cash, our dream vacation to Italy for our twentieth anniversary.

Another blessing that came our way was in the area of housing. Daphne's parents had, for several years, worked in short-term missions. They helped storm-ravaged Haitians, ministered to folks in the frozen badlands of Alaska, worked alongside ministries in the Philippines, and several other places. As we did every year, we had Thanksgiving dinner at their house, but Thanksgiving of 2013 would be different. They told us they had an announcement to make. They felt like God was calling them to a more permanent role in missionary work. They made us the offer to move into their fully-furnished house and pay their mortgage (which was half of what we paid), so that they could be free to do the work God had for them. Of course, we took them up on the offer, and I started mentally calculating how much more money we would have.

But God, obviously, had other plans. More on that in a moment.

Now, on to Ileana…

It was a Thursday in September 2014. I was at work, and it was a little before lunch time. I was on my way into the church's auditorium, which required me to walk through the front office area, and there sat my good friend Ricky. He was there to take his son, one of my co-workers, to lunch.

"Hey, man! I'm glad I caught you. I have a question," he said. "I've always wondered… why don't you play upright bass anymore?"

(A little backstory on Ricky and me: my degree is in music. I was a string bass major, and I had done a good bit of upright bass playing in the classical and jazz worlds. Ricky and his wife Carol came to a few of my concerts. I rebuilt one of my electric basses on his living room floor, while house-sitting for him. He was always supportive of me, no matter what I was doing.)

"I never owned a bass. I always used a school instrument."

"That's what I thought. What does one of those things cost?"

"Well…" I answered, "you can get a cheap plywood bass for under a grand."

"What do *you* want?" He replied.

(More backstory: at that point, my Facebook profile picture had been an upright bass for almost four years. Daphne was constantly asking me to update that picture and my response was always, "When I get a bass, I'll change it.")

As if it were over-rehearsed, my reply came out, flowing with the same sense of excitement as little

Ralphie Parker, describing his much-anticipated Red Ryder BB gun with a compass in the stock, and this thing which tells time.

"I'd want a fully-carved Eastern European gamba-styled bass."

He questioned further. "What do *those* cost?"

"Unless you find someone desperate for cash, they start at around three or four grand, and they just go up from there."

His reply floored me. "Hmmm. Well, I can't promise I can do that, but God has put you on my heart. I have a year-end bonus coming up, and I want to help you buy one."

What?! For twenty-three years, I've wanted one of these basses, and my dream was finally becoming a reality.

"Well, I'll promise you this," I replied, trying to not get too emotional, "Whatever you will give to me, if it's not enough for what I want, I'll put it into a savings account, and when I have enough to get what I want, I'll buy it. I will not use your money for anything else."

"Good deal," he said, as his son showed up, and they walked out of the building together.

I was on cloud nine! I was so incredibly thankful for what God was setting up that I went around and told everyone in the building. I was so overwhelmed with God's goodness and Ricky's generosity that, for the rest of the day, I couldn't concentrate on my work.

A couple weeks later, Ricky gave me a check for twenty-five hundred dollars! I landed another video job, and was able to put together, after my tithe, about thirty-three hundred dollars. On October 13, 2014, I purchased my beautiful fully-carved Eastern European gamba-styled upright bass. I paid $3,336 for her. That's right. Out-of-pocket costs were a whopping thirty-six dollars!

At this point, it is worth noting a couple of other interesting threads woven into the fabric that is our story. First, all roads lead to Houston. "Linda" was purchased there, as was Daphne's SUV. Katie's stem cell transplant and subsequent treatments for graft versus host disease were there. It's also the city in which I found my upright bass. And speaking of that, "Linda's" purchase was in direct connection to blessings we received after supporting two different missionary works in Romania... which is where my bass was made! I named her "Ileana," which is a Romanian name for "bright one," so that I could always use her story to be a bright light of faith to those willing to listen to her (my) awesome story.

Anyway, getting back to the day I spoke with Ricky. Driving home from work, I did what every Christian does when he or she gets a blessing: I thanked God for it and prayed He would bless the giver. Right in the middle of all of this, God stopped me, dead in my tracks. I sensed Him speaking to me.

"In the grand scheme of things, whether or not you own an upright bass is completely immaterial. But if I can get this thing to you, in this way, just know, you can trust me with anything."

I was speechless. The God of all creation was speaking directly to me, telling me *I* could trust *Him* with *anything*. Immediately, my mind went to Daphne, and her regrets over backing off of women's ministry. (A little more backstory on Daphne's situation: at this point, she was really missing women's ministry, and all of our debt, minus the student loans, was gone. A few conversations had already taken place about her quitting her job, or going part-time, so that she could devote more time to women's ministry.) My thought was that this was for her, to free her from her job, so that she'd have time to do what was in her heart.

When I got home, I told her the incredible story of the bass, and what God had spoken. I told her I was fine with her going part-time, or even quitting if she wanted, that God had blessed us so much that maybe this was all just for her. We began to plan how she'd change her work life to make more time for her ministry life.

Fast-forward to Monday, April 13, 2015. I had just gotten home from taking Katie to get lab work done, and then to school, and then a personal errand. As I was letting Roxy, our dog, out, Daphne called me, telling me about Katie's platelet count, and the dire situation she was facing.

Obviously, I was shaken. I called Roxy back in, put her in her kennel, and headed to the hospital. I began to cry. I began to beg God to not let my baby girl die. I posted something on Facebook about what was happening and asking people to pray. I began to get nervous and really scared.

I pulled into the parking lot of Women's and Children's Hospital. I turned off the ignition and touched the door handle to get out and at that very moment, God brought back the memory of the upright bass, my beloved Ileana, and how He orchestrated her purchase. He then posed a question to me, with words I'll never forget:

"Do you still trust Me?"

In that moment, I realized I was the fortunate victim of the most Divine "gotcha" question ever. God was using my own logic against me in the most wonderful way. He set up all the blessings, all the dissolved debt, all the provision, for this moment in time.

"Lord, You've helped us get out of all that debt. I've been bragging on You for a year and a half. The whole Internet knows that. If, all of a sudden, I say that I don't trust You, then I'm the worst Christian ever. I'm the worst child You've ever had. Yes, God. I trust You. I trust You with everything. I trust You with my family. I trust You with Katie."

Even after Katie's diagnosis and treatment, the blessings didn't end. During Katie's transplant days, the church board gave me five thousand dollars and a four-month paid sabbatical so I could just be with her and Daphne. A Cajun comedian did a huge benefit show for us, bringing in thousands of dollars. Knowing we'd need to make countless trips back and forth to Houston, and knowing Daphne's SUV was up in age, I asked God for ten thousand dollars to buy a new vehicle, but I didn't tell a soul. Daphne went to a women's event back at our church, where she was honored for the ordeal we were facing, and several hundred ladies there all prayed for her and us. Upon witnessing all of this, a woman in attendance went home later that night and told her husband, and they donated ten thousand dollars to us! Donations poured in from all over the world. After Katie went back into the hospital, I got a job, working about six hours a week, that paid more than my first forty-hour job. A dear friend (with an amazing healing/faith story all her own) organized a benefit for us at the local Harley-Davidson dealership. We shattered all records, pulling in roughly ten times the normal amount of any benefit they had ever hosted!

At that same benefit a friend of mine walked up to me and handed me a check for ten thousand dollars to cover seven months of rent and expenses (Houston Medical Center is crazy expensive). I'll never forget our conversation.

I told him I was so thankful for the gift and that receiving it was one of the most humbling things I've ever had to do. He then asked, "How long have you been in ministry?"

"About twenty years, off and on, full-time," I replied.

"Well, you've always gotten paid by people giving as unto the Lord. It's just always come through a ministry organization. But now, you're ministering to your family, full-time, and we see that, and we want to support you directly, but we're still giving as unto the Lord."

The weight of that statement still haunts me to this day. I always viewed my money coming from holy money (tithes and offerings), but I also saw it as *my* money, money that I worked forty to fifty hours each week to get. But this money was different. This money was meant for a specific purpose, and that purpose was far above my own desires for it. This money was meant for me to use for someone else: my sweet Katie.

But the reality is that *all* of the money was for Katie. It was for us to use to be with her, to care for her, and to ease the burden of worrying about our own finances so that we could focus every bit of our energy on her.

So even during the darkest moments any parent could face, we were blessed. We were blessed beyond what we could ask or think. Our needs were met. Our financial burdens were never an issue. And I attribute all of that to one thing: my response to God, that Monday morning in my car, on Day One of Katie's first trip to the hospital. I believe God's Divine "gotcha" question was my test. I had the choice to tell Him I still trusted Him, and I had the choice to curse Him, seeing only my hurt and fears for my child. It may be one of the only times in my entire life that I chose well.

With all that said, I've had a few observations about blessings. One of the biggest mistakes we often make is that we think the blessings are for us, whether they are financial, spiritual, or relational. One of the biggest lessons about blessings we've learned is this: not every blessing is for us, and sometimes, blessings received are ultimately for someone else.

All of the debt paid off, all of the provisions God had for us, and the housing situation (we sold our house in July 2015, right before going to Houston for Katie's transplant) were not for us, but for Katie. God allowed us to get out of debt and sell our house so we could be instantly mobile to ensure her best care, not just in a medical capacity, but also by being as close to a family unit as we could possibly be. We were, quite literally, set free from any financial responsibilities for the first time in almost ten years! Not only did we not have a mortgage, but we had sold everything to move into a fully-furnished house. Everything we owned, outside of our cars, fit into an 8x10 trailer and the back of a pickup truck. God was setting us up to just focus on Katie and what she needed, and that's just what we did.

As for Daphne's work, it was God's provision for our church for her to leave when she did. It was tough on the department when I left in February 2016, but it would have been even worse for the media department to lose *two* employees at once. Even the fact that she worked for and with me for seven years is something that God used in Katie's situation. All those years of teamwork in a creative environment helped us to work together as a team to provide for Katie's care.

On the relational front, we were able to meet and minister to dozens of families faced with dire circumstances. As stated in Chapter One, even the doctors knew we were believers. Obviously, we in no way feel like all this happened to Katie just to get us in

228

relationship with other people, but God still used us to be an encouragement to them, to be a light in some very dark places, to be His voice to those hurting. Not only patients, but we also had the opportunity, on a few occasions, to share our faith with the medical teams at Texas Children's Hospital.

Yes, we have been blessed.

Blessed to have our needs met.

Blessed to have wonderful relationships.

Blessed to know the provision of an infinitely-resourced God.

Blessed for others' sakes. And that's the biggest blessing of all.

THE PROBLEM WITH
PROBLEM-SOLVING
Richard

We are not necessarily doubting that God will do the best
for us; we are wondering how painful the best will turn
out to be.
- C.S. Lewis, *The Letters of C.S.Lewis*

In school, we all learned about the basic questions involved with information-gathering or problem-solving. "The Five Ws and Sometimes How" and the since-minted-after-I-graduated "5W1H" represent how we can go about getting the information we need to make informed decisions, or write a story or report. They are:

Who? What? When? Where? Why? and How?

Those five questions are the backbone of journalism, research, and police investigations. In fact, a report isn't considered complete unless it answers the first five questions.

But what if those questions can't be answered? What if, after your research, you come to no conclusion, other than "we live in a fallen world"? What if you are faced with such a dire situation that merely fact-finding doesn't bring the peace for which you are so desperately looking?

Welcome to our lives.

Obviously, Katie's situation made no sense. She was the very picture of health until she wasn't. She was

233

our soccer star. Her volleyball serve was almost unanswerable by her middle-school opponents. Words such as "guns," "boot," and "cannon" were often used to describe her strength on the field or on the court. The girl had energy like no one else, and physical agility that often sent boys crying to the teacher during co-ed recesses or sports times.

Nonetheless, there we were, facing a sickness that could only be cured with drastic measures. Expensive, lengthy, exasperating, heart-breaking measures, about which none of us had ever heard.

I like to think of myself as being mainly ruled by logic. Some may disagree with my self-assessment, but that is another subject for another day. But God often speaks to me through my own logic and mental processes. He knows I'm a thinker and an analyzer, so He gives me thoughts that take a long time to process. Maybe it was His way of giving me much-needed distractions. Or maybe He was trying to give me long-lasting hope.

So as I, naturally, started processing Katie's situation through my own logic, those questions started coming up in my mind; though the "why" plagued me the most. The more I pondered the questions, the more I came up with ways to deal with what we were facing.

Let's consider these questions, although not in their journalistic order, but rather in the way I came about my conclusions. Because the "why?" question was so pervasive, I began there.

Why would this happen to an innocent girl? Why would this happen to us? All we've ever done is try to serve God, so, why is this happening? Those are obvious questions, but we tried our best not to ask them, for several reasons.

Firstly, it's a question that will never get answered sufficiently. Suppose you and I were in a conversation, and I asked you, "Why did you wear that blue shirt today?"

To this you replied, "Because it's my favorite color."

"Why?"

"Because, it reminds me of a beautiful sky and placid water."

"Why?"

"Because... water is... blue and... the sky is... blue."

"Why?"

With a puzzled look on your face, you are now needing to go into the science-heavy laws of refraction, sunlight effects on water vapor, and stuff you never even knew you knew. At that point, I would ask the question, yet again. At some point, you would realize that there is *nothing* you could say that would make me stop asking. It's the question version of trumping all of your childhood friends trying to count to infinity. They say "infinity," and you reply with "infinity plus one." It never adds up. It never gets solved. It never ends.

Another reason we have chosen not to ask "why?" is this: even if we know why, it wouldn't change the facts. Katie would have been sick, whether we understood it, knew why it happened, or had definitive answers to any other questions we could have asked. No amount of inquisitiveness could change the fact that our little girl faced what not many others face. We could know every single detail of why it happened, but Katie still would have found herself in the exact same situation, and it would have been just as hard for us, and it would still leave us asking that same one-word question.

Thirdly, when we look at Scripture, we see that ours is a faith journey, not a sighted one. 2 Corinthians 5:7 says that we walk by faith, and not by sight. We are not called to see it all but rather to trust, to have faith in

ıe Who does. Hebrews 11:6 tells us that, without
t's impossible to please God. If we continually
n "why," then are we not guilty of walking by
what is seen, and not by what we believe? We are
choosing to walk by something that runs the risk of
displeasing God in the process, which leads me to the
next point…

If we elevate our need to know why above the
sovereignty of God, then we have made an idol of our
desire for knowledge. There is no other way to put this.
God hates idolatry. It's found all over the Bible. Simply
put, an idol is something you put before, place more
emphasis on, think about more, or worship more than
God Himself.

I began to think about Romans 8:28 (NIV),
which says, "And we know that in all things God works
for the good of those who love him, who have been
called according to his purpose." We *love* to quote that
verse, because it gives us a feeling of invincibility, like we
can do anything, like there are no barriers from
achieving anything that is in our hearts. *But that verse caps
off a whole section on suffering.* As you read Romans
8:18-30, you realize Paul was writing about present
suffering and future glory, and that, in that suffering,
God is still at work. With that in mind, I came up with
more appropriate questions to ask.

The first one was this: "What?"

I began to ask, "God, what do You want to do in
me? What do You want to do in Katie? In Daphne? In
Kylie (halfway around the world, in another country)?
What do You want to do in my family?" Knowing that
God wants to work continually in the lives of His people,
and knowing that the only way to truly develop the
character of God is through suffering, I began to
embrace this question, and I asked it almost daily. I
began to look for ways to see God at work in me, in my

wife, and in my girls. And any time you begin to look for ways God is moving, He always shows up, and shows up *big*. I began to see how my wife was such a servant. I began to see how Katie was so incredibly resilient in the face of fear, torment, and pain. I began to see how Kylie was growing in her faith and knowledge. I began to see my three girls becoming more like Jesus.

This led me to ask the "who?" question. "God, who will You reach through Katie's story? Who will You touch through us, here at the hospital, through social media, through Daphne's blog posts, through my music gigs, through the way You are giving us grace and sustaining us through all of this?" This situation, although completely terrible, gave us a platform to share our faith with other families at Texas Children's Hospital, and other people with whom we would come into contact. It also gave me the chance to share our faith with the medical staff on many occasions. Almost everyone I talked to at TCH, for any length of time, knew about Katie, and it opened the door for me to speak about the goodness of God through a tremendously difficult season.

I also began to ask the "how?" question. "God, how are You going to glorify Yourself in me? How are You going to glorify Yourself in my family? How are You going to glorify Yourself in this situation?" I began to look for opportunities not only to share my faith, but also to glorify God in the midst of the trial. I looked for good things happening, for prayers answered, for others' successes, for *our* successes. Katie having a great physical therapy session wasn't only about a good physical therapy session. It also became about how God was working in her body. Many times, conversations with her turned to faith and then into faith statements. She had Scriptures posted on her wall, proclaiming who she was oclaiming His strength working through her, His glory in and through her.

her way we began to see the "how?" answered was by seeing God's grace in the situation. The following is an excerpt of Daphne's journal on the subject:

Grace

I've heard this phrase a lot lately from people... that God would grant us "enough grace" or "more grace" to get through each day during this time.

It's not the first I've heard of this. In fact, I've prayed it for other people, myself. It's just kind of a thing we, as Christians, pray. It's something we sing... "Your grace is enough..." It's in so many of our worship songs. It's sorta like a Christian catch-phrase.

But I didn't grasp what it even meant until now.

We often get grace and mercy confused. This is the best explanation of the difference that I've found:

Mercy is NOT getting what we deserve; grace is GETTING what we do not deserve.

Mercy: God saves me from punishment and death that I deserve because of sin.
Grace: God shows His kindness and favor to me despite the fact that I don't deserve it.

Grace has been described as unmerited favor. What a wonderful thought! It can't be earned, but God just freely gives it to us, like the good Father that He is. An earthly father would have issues with giving his child kindness, love, gifts, and favor. If the child were disobedient, disrespectful, and the like, an earthly father would have a very hard time with this. Eventually, an earthly father would grant grace, but only after he got over whatever the child did or continued to do. But God's not like that. Despite what we do as His children, He grants us grace, when we faithfully follow Him.

So, what does it mean for God to grant us "enough" grace or "more" grace.

There will always be "enough" grace for us. Grace has always been around for us and God continues to grant us the grace we need for each day.

From the beginning of time, grace was there... enough grace... and more grace.

Grace is already there before our circumstance arrives.

We pray for more grace when we're going through hard times. I now understand that.

There are times that we need more grace from God, times where we have nothing else and can only rely on the grace of God to get us through to the next day, times where we need more favor, times where we just simply need God to work things out for us even when we don't know what those things are. That's "more" grace.

Right now, we need more grace. The amazing thing is, the grace we need was already here, waiting for us to arrive at this time in our lives. God knew this time would come, and we can see His hand in so many areas, working things out for us.

239

The grace that each of us needs for different times in our lives is always there. It's God's grace that sustains us in hard times. And, in those hard times, our spirits are sensitive to His and our eyes are more open to see His hand in it all. We see Him working out even the smallest details to create the bigger picture where He is ultimately glorified. I think we also see God's grace more clearly displayed when we come to a point in our lives that we have fully surrendered to His ways, when we have no control over anything and all we can do is rely on Him. It's when we give up our control that He can display His very sufficient grace. It's when we make Him all that we need and come to realize who He is. That's when giving up control and letting God do His work is easier.

Not only is God love, but He is also grace. It's in His character and a part of who He is.

When I look back on the last few months, I see how God has worked out so many details and given us such favor in different areas to get us to where we are now. And, the awesome thing is... His grace will continue to be enough and He will extend us more grace in the coming weeks, months, and years. Because He sees what's ahead and the grace we need awaits us in the moments set before us.

After you have suffered for a little while, the God of grace who has called you [to His everlasting presence]through Jesus the Anointed will restore you, support you, strengthen you, and ground you. (1 Peter 5:10 VOICE)

What a beautiful and eloquent way to see that God is working out the "how" by simply giving us grace through the hardest season through which we've ever walked!

240

So with all of that said, let's go back to the "why?" question. The thing I began to realize through all of this is that asking "why?" makes it all about us, while asking "what?," "who?," and "how?" makes it all about Him. Asking "why?" comes from a place of selfishness, a place where we tend to make false assumptions about God and His character. It's almost as if we are telling God we don't deserve bad things to happen, that we're more special than that. It's almost as if we are telling God to let bad stuff happen to other people we think aren't as good as us. It's almost as if we are telling God that, although sin entered into the world by the disobedience of Adam and Eve, it's somehow *His* fault for not just stopping the consequences. Asking "*What* do You want to do in me?" is built on the assumption (faith) that He *is* going to do something. Asking "*Who* are You going to reach?" is based in the assumption (faith) that He *is* going to reach someone. Asking "*How* are you going to glorify Yourself?" is based in the assumption (faith) that He *is* going to glorify Himself.

Another thing to consider about the "why?" question is this: it's already been answered.

John 9:1-7 (NIV) says this:

> *As he went along, he saw a man blind from birth. His disciples asked him, "Rabbi, who sinned, this man or his parents, that he was born blind?"* (Even then, talking straight to Jesus, the "why" was about something someone had done. It was about them and not Him.) *"Neither this man nor his parents sinned," said Jesus, "but this happened so that the works of God might be displayed in him. As long as it is day, we must do the works of him who sent me. Night is coming, when no one can work. While I am in the world, I am the light of the world." After saying this, he spit on the ground, made some mud with the saliva, and put it on the man's eyes.*

"Go," he told him, "wash in the Pool of Siloam." So the man went and washed, and came home seeing.

Notice that the people asking Jesus the question of who sinned were His disciples. This was not just another situation where the Pharisees were out to get Him. It was a legitimate question asked by His closest followers. If we use His response as our example of how to respond, then the answer to the "why?" is quite simple, taking into consideration two facts:

FACT ONE: This did not happen because of my sin, Daphne's sin, Katie's sin, or Kylie's sin. God does not punish us for not meeting His standards. He allowed Jesus to take that on.

FACT TWO: God did not cause this but allowed it to happen to Katie (and to us) so that He could be glorified, so that the works of God could be displayed in us. And as long as it is day, He (we) was (are) here to do the work of the Father.

The first fact shows the goodness of God. The second shows our response to that goodness. In other words, God allowed Christ to take on sickness and sin through the beating and death of His Son, Jesus. It's our job to make that known while we still have breath in our lungs, even though we are suffering.

Another question in the formula is that of the "when?" dilemma. Of course, we looked to God to heal Katie. We wanted her healed in this life more than anything. She firmly believed God would heal her in the way we all expected and that she would use that healing as a platform to share her testimony with thousands of people, mostly teenaged girls. But her healing didn't happen in that way. We had to trust in God's timing, in God's perfect plan, and in God's infinite wisdom.

But, continually asking "when?" can reveal the heart of someone who lacks patience. Just as the "why?"

242

can reveal idolatry in the heart, asking "w
that the person isn't really trusting God's
want things done on their own schedule ¿
willing simply to wait on God. Some could a._
question is based on extreme faith, *knowing* that God ..
work, but I would surmise that, most of the time, it is a
sign of spiritual immaturity. Just as a child can't wait to
open a present, or they can't simply be told to wait, so is
the immature Christ-follower. Also, continuing to ask
"when?" can reveal that the person is more concerned
with the end result, and not the process of becoming
mature.

Another thing to consider when asking the
"when?" question is this: James 4:14 describes our lives
as but a vapor, a mist that appears for a little while and
then vanishes. With that in mind, in the light of eternity,
with our lives as a vapor, being impatient is like having
an incredible short-sighted mindset.

For example, let's say I am building some sort of
model that takes a very long time to assemble, with lots
of small, intricate pieces, and I had one particular part
that required the use of quick-dry cement. The time it
takes for that cement to dry would be roughly twenty
seconds, but I complain about the twenty seconds I have
to wait, even though the model takes me three months to
complete. It would be silly to focus that much energy on
the cement, knowing it was just a sliver of time
compared to the whole process.

The same can be said of our lives and of events
occurring in them. In the light of eternity, our lives aren't
even the thickness of a sheet of paper. They aren't even
the thickness of the layer of molecules that makes up the
surface of the paper! So a particular event in our lives
wouldn't even be but a fraction of that surface. Why get
so bogged down in continually wondering when the
miracle is coming when you will have all of eternity to

celebrate Christ's victory over Death, Hell, and the Grave?

In other words, as incredible as having Katie healed in this life would have been, it would still be a temporary bandage on a larger issue, and that is this: there is an appointed time for man to die, and then the judgment. The most important thing is that Katie knew Jesus and that she is now in Heaven with Him, and that is the place we all aspire to be. And just like it is our responsibility to trust and not walk by sight, it was our responsibility to trust and not wonder when.

The last problem-solving question is that of "where?". In the light of my findings on the "when?" question, I had to come to a point of realization that Katie's healing may not happen in this life but rather by crossing into eternity. As much as I wanted to see her healed here, I had to trust that her healing was ultimately up to God's sovereignty, wisdom, and plan. I had to come to the realization that, no matter what happened, Katie won. If God chose to heal her, she won. If God chose to take her, she *really* won! As much as I miss my beautiful girl, as much as I continue to grieve her loss, as much as I wish her to be here with me, the fact is that she is now in God's presence and she would *never* want to come back. Her suffering is over. She ran her race, the one we tried our best to prepare her for since before she was born. We tried so desperately, with every medical intervention known to man, to keep her here, continuing to run it. But she finished, and she finished strong.

Katie won.

It's interesting to me that, even though we were trusting God, even though we were seeing Him move in our lives, situation, and sphere of influence, I still had nagging thoughts of unanswered questions. At one point, I even said this:

"When I get to Heaven, I've got questions."

The self-reaction to my statement startled me a little. Right after saying that, my first reaction was, "No you won't."

Let me explain.

By the time I get to Heaven, none of those questions will matter. The "what?," the "when?," the "where?," and the "how?" will be passed, the "why?" will be all about God's love for us, and my worship of Him. The sliver of time that was my life will have occurred and vaporized, and I will be left with an eternity consumed in God's presence, with my Katie and all of the saints "who" have gone before and after us. Those questions won't matter. They will have long-since melted away with my first glance at our unlimitedly-faceted God. For the rest of the future, for the rest of forever, for the eternal rest of a life lived for God, so shall my life be.

So those are the questions and their answers I've come up with. But there is one more statement that, I believe, bears noting. In our earthly thinking, we want those answers. We want those solutions to problems that are bigger than us.

We want to problem-solve our way through it all.

But, the problem with problem-solving is that it's not our problem to solve. None of this was ever meant to be met with our fix. God never intended us to face any of this in our own earthly wisdom, strength, understanding, or logic. In reality, *no* problem was ever meant for us to handle that way. In Matthew 11:28-30, Jesus promised us that if we are burdened and heavy-laden, that we could take His light yoke upon ourselves, that we could learn from Him, and that He would give our weary souls rest. When we place our faith in Him, when we trust that He is good and is always working on our behalf, we take ourselves out of the problem-solver

245

role, and place ourselves at the feet of Him Who has it all worked out for us.

We are His. The problem is His. We just have to put our trust and faith in the Great Divine Problem-Solver.

WORTH IT
Richard

What would cause us to immerse ourselves into the intricate details about bone marrow, transplants, blood, diseases, and the like? What would cause me to stop my life, end my career, and move my family to another state, without any guarantees of income, housing, or the future? What would cause Daphne to end her career as well, drop everything, leave relationships behind, and fall into relative obscurity in a foreign city?

Our child.

The best way I could describe it is this: Katie was worth it. She was worth the sacrifices. She was worth pain, tears, sleeplessness, stress, anxiety, labor, and any other thing we could have ever done for her or felt for her. She had our hearts before she was even born, and she was an amazing young woman, but even if she had never accomplished anything with her life, she would still be worth it.

Her worth was not determined by what she gave to us. It wasn't determined by how much she made us laugh, how much she cared for other people, how pretty she was, how athletic she was, or any other attribute we can ascribe to her. She truly was all those things, but her worth was solely based on the fact that she was created in God's own image, and that she was loved by her Creator.

The honest truth is this: we are *all* worth it. Sometimes we fail to see that because we don't have people in our lives who are willing to declare our worth to us.

But God knows your worth.

Perhaps no one has ever told you that you have worth. Maybe you, at one time, felt a sense of worth, but life has convinced you otherwise. Nothing could be farther from the truth!

I do not ever want to give the connotation that I am comparing myself to Jesus, but I desperately want to be like Him. If you think about our family's story, and how we responded, it is a reflection of how God responds to us. I don't say this in a boastful fashion, but we have no regrets for how we dealt with Katie's situation, because I can honestly say I did what I think Jesus would have done.

Jesus willingly left the comforts and glory of Heaven, to go to a world where He knew death awaited Him. He willingly took on our sickness, burdens, and sin. He gave His very life so we could live, and in so doing, became our best friend and advocate. And that's exactly what we tried to do.

Why did we do it? Because of Katie's worth to us. Why did He do it? Because of our worth to God. Because of *your* worth to God.

God loves each one of us so much and sees so much worth in all of us that He was willing to part with His own Son so that we could know Him. But ever since the earliest days of mankind, there has been a disconnect between God and man because of man's selfishness.

The following is a post in Daphne's journal from August 7th, 2017, the day before my fiftieth birthday. The day before my first birthday without my Katie. Notice the hurt in Daphne's "voice" as she describes life without Katie:

"A Letter to My Daughter"

My sweet girl,

It's been over three weeks since I've heard your voice. I remember your precious voice in our last phone conversation, where you called me at 1:00 am to bring you homemade sweet tea, a true southern belle until the very end. I didn't know that was the last time you would call me. I often re-read our last text conversations and scroll through pictures and videos of you on my phone. I replay the last conversations with you over and over again in my head, trying to remember everything we said to each other, counting how many times I said that I loved you and how proud I was of you, and wishing I could tell you so much more. Our last moments together were too short. I hope you truly knew how much your daddy and I loved you. We did everything we knew to keep you here with us, to help you fight the hardest battle I've seen anyone ever have to fight. I ask myself if we could've done anything else, anything more. But I come up with the same answer: We did everything. It's simply not right and not fair. I get angry when I think about all the enemy has stolen from you and us.

I truly believed that you were the one who would make it through this. There are definitely a million thoughts and questions that continue to go through my mind on a daily basis, and emotions that are all over the place in regards to "why." Even though I know there are no answers, the

251

questions and confusion keep rising up. I believed God would heal you here on earth. I saw His hand pulling you through so many obstacles that even amazed the doctors. "Resilient" is the word that was used to describe you. Each time you were faced with yet another issue, you came through it.

I miss you terribly. There isn't a day, an hour, that goes by that I don't think about you. The weight on my chest seems unbearable at times. It hurts so bad. I cry every day and in the moments I'm not crying, I feel guilty... guilty that I'm doing everyday stuff, guilty that I'm living, guilty for any moments I'm not thinking about you. What I wouldn't give to snuggle with you in the bed again, to hold your hand, to have another conversation, to just be next to you.

The hole you've left in our lives is enormous. From the time you came into our lives, we were changed for the better. I think about how we were inseparable when you were a baby. You would cry for hours when I wasn't around. At the time, it exhausted me. But now I cherish the moments when I bounced you up and down on my hip, rocked you, napped with you, held you. You finally gained your independence and you were a force to be reckoned with always. I love that about you. Even these last years, you stood up for yourself regarding your care. The strength you showed was incredible, physically and mentally.

I worry about your daddy and your sister. I don't want them to hurt. I want them to be okay, just like I always wanted you to be. They loved you so much. Our family is not the same without you, but we are still a family. We look different without you.

So, how do we go on? That's been the question of each day. How do we move on? Moving on doesn't even seem like an option. It seems impossible. My prayer each day has been simple: "Jesus, help me."

I know that you're up in Heaven, worshiping God in all His glory. I try to think about what it was like when you took that last breath and finally saw Jesus. I imagine you running into His arms, safe and sound.

I know that you will never read this letter. But I needed to write it.

I love you, sweet girl. The fact that God chose me to be your mama has been an honor and a blessing. I know that you would be sad that we are sad right now. You hated what all this did to us and would always apologize for stuff that was never your fault. I can hear you apologizing now, just like you would apologize to the doctors when you would code and they would have to do extra work. Even that showed your heart. You always worried about everyone else. You cared and loved everyone. And you were loved by so many.

Attempting to close out this letter crushes me, so I won't.

I can't wait to see you again.

Mama

Beautiful words from a mother who would have gone to the grave itself to save her girl. Yet another perfect picture of the love of God for us. God longs to be in relationship with us. God longs to be in relationship with *you.* Just as we did everything we knew to keep Katie with us, so has God done everything He could to keep you in relationship with Him. Jesus died so that you might live.

One of the reasons Daphne and I wrote this book was to preserve Katie's legacy. We want the world to know how incredible she was. We want everyone to understand the magnitude of her suffering and how she dealt with it. We want everyone to know about her unyielding faith in the God she so loved.

Katie longed to please God with everything she had in her. She firmly believed her story would be told to thousands of people, and that she would have the opportunity to lead them to Christ. She never got to see that during her time on Earth.

But here you are, reading the epilogue of the book about her family's story.

If you don't know Jesus, Katie would be so thrilled to have you decide to follow Him, especially after reading our story. There is no better way to honor her memory than for you to consider giving your life to the One who sees, in you, so much worthiness of His love that He was willing to be brutally beaten, mocked, and executed for your sake. He left Heaven so you could enter it. He walked through Hell so you could escape it.

Jesus was Katie's everything. He wants to become yours, as well.

Please, in all sincerity, pray this to God right now:

God, I know that I need you. I know that I am a sinner, and that my sin keeps me from You. I don't want to be apart from You any longer. I renounce my selfish lifestyle, and from this moment on, I choose to follow Jesus. I choose to serve Him, and to live for Him. I don't live for myself any longer. Please, help me to live for You. I receive Your forgiveness of my sin, and I thank you that I am now a new creation in Christ, and that I have eternal life. Thank you for saving me. In Jesus' name, I pray. Amen.

Amen, indeed. If you meant that prayer in your heart, you have every right to know, beyond a shadow of a doubt, that you have been forgiven, and that you are no longer the same person. You are now free from sin, and God will begin working in you, changing you from the inside out, giving you faith to trust in Him, and giving you strength to live for Him.

Thank you for letting our story be a factor in your decision. Thank you for letting us lead you to Jesus. We'd love to know about it. We'd love to know how our precious daughter's story influenced your decision to become a fellow follower of Christ. Please email us at info@wearestillrising.com. We want to celebrate with you and help you in your new walk with Christ.

The Bible says in Luke 15:7 that all of Heaven is rejoicing because of your decision to follow Jesus. And guess what?

That includes Katie.

The Still Rising Foundation resources ministry-minded young women and serves families of pediatric bone marrow transplant patients, thus, honoring the memory of Katie Gaspard.

After a lengthy battle with a rare blood disease and its complications, Katie Gaspard, at the age of sixteen, passed from this life on July 20, 2017.

Katie's life was one well-lived. Even in the face of overwhelming circumstances and tremendous pain, she was fearless. At a time when she could have had a completely inward focus, Katie remained unselfish, loving, and compassionate towards others, their trials, and their suffering.

Even as a young child, Katie's greatest desire was to tell others about Jesus. She planned to attend a ministry school, in preparation for whatever God called her to do. One of Katie's greatest joys in her short life was attending Christian camps and conferences.

As her parents, we want to honor her memory, striving to do our very best to make her story known to all who will listen, and to continue her legacy of making Jesus famous. Our scholarship fund provides resources to young women who aspire to serve in ministry. Similarly, we also offer scholarships for young women to attend the same types of camps and conventions Katie enjoyed so much.

While inpatient at Texas Children's Hospital, we saw a tremendous need in the lives of fellow bone marrow transplant families. It is our mission to serve those families in whatever capacity we are able, as often as we are able.

You, too, can be a part of honoring Katie's legacy. For more information, visit www.wearestillrising.com.